"*Twenty-volume folios
will never make a revolution.
It's the little pocket pamphlets
that are to be feared.*"
Voltaire

FIELD (#**8**) NOTES

CASEY PLETT

On Community

BIBLIOASIS

Windsor, Ontario

FIRST EDITION
10 9 8 7 6 5 4 3 2 1

Library and Archives Canada Cataloguing in Publication
Title: On community / Casey Plett.
Names: Plett, Casey, author.
Series: Field notes (Biblioasis) ; #8
Description: Series statement: Field notes; #8
Identifiers: Canadiana (print) 20230509975 | Canadiana (ebook) 20230509991
    ISBN 9781771965774 (softcover) | ISBN 9781771965781 (EPUB)
Subjects: LCSH: Communities. | LCSH: Community life. | LCSH: Social
    participation.
Classification: LCC HM756 .P54 2023 | DDC 307—dc23

Edited by Daniel Wells
Copyedited by John Sweet
Typeset by Vanessa Stauffer
Series designed by Ingrid Paulson

Published with the generous assistance of the Canada Council for the Arts,
which last year invested $153 million to bring the arts to Canadians throughout
the country, and the financial support of the Government of Canada. Biblioasis
also acknowledges the support of the Ontario Arts Council (OAC), an agency of
the Government of Ontario, which last year funded 1,709 individual artists
and 1,078 organizations in 204 communities across Ontario, for a total of
$52.1 million, and the contribution of the Government of Ontario through the
Ontario Book Publishing Tax Credit and Ontario Creates.

PRINTED AND BOUND IN CANADA

For my grandfather Gerry Doerksen,
who passed away as I was writing this
and who lived much of his life as a pillar
of his own communities

I hope you might enjoy this,
wherever it now may find you

Rest in peace

Nothing is sweet or easy about community. Community is a fellowship of people who do not hide their joys and sorrows but make them visible to each other as a gesture of hope.

Henri Nouwen

Over time, I had learned that the strength of a close-knit social group lies in its ability to compartmentalize.

Rawi Hage,
"The Iconoclast," *Stray Dogs*

We sometimes make compromises, invite poison into our lives, and it can't be helped.

Venita Blackburn,
"Blood, Guts, and Bile,"
How to Wrestle a Girl

If my experiences in gay bars have been disappointing, what I wouldn't want to lose is the expectation of a better night.

Jeremy Atherton Lin, *Gay Bar: Why We Went Out*

Sodden, satisfied, you
return, take the body,
push its palms up under
your shirt. You say *I am
now safe* but the body narrows
against the window,
folds over the kitchen
sink rubbing small
ceramic cups, old church
mugs after midnight,
the curtains worn blue
& floating, back
& forth like whispers.
    The body squints; a ghost cycled in the garden.

Sarah Ens, "Wuthering:
A Comprehensive Guide,"
The World Is Mostly Sky

I.

Assumptions (1)

WHEN I WAS a kid, I lived in a small town. It's a dot on the Canadian Prairies, in the Pembina Valley region of Southern Manitoba. I wasn't well-liked; I didn't get along with most other children. I moved away with my mom and stepdad after grade five.

A decade afterwards, I went back to visit. I went to a party with a boy, the only friend I'd kept in touch with. It was the kind of party where guys were mean and the kitchen counter was covered with alcohol. We walked in and one of the guys pointed at me. "Who the *fuck* is that?"

"It's cool, he's from here," said my old friend.

And that took care of that.

I've moved often in my thirty-six years of life—ten times, as of now. And often I've returned to visit a community in which I once lived, and said those words, "I'm from here." Sometimes it doesn't mean anything. But it meant something, that night, at that party.

MEANWHILE, ONE TOWN over, my uncle taught in the schools. He'd grown up elsewhere, in the Steinbach area, about an hour away. One day, he told me of his adopted town, "I've lived there twenty years and I still don't feel like I'm *from* there."

Both the Pembina Valley and the Steinbach region are overwhelmingly made up of people like my family: Mennonites descended from Low German–speaking communities who emigrated from eastern Europe between the 1870s and 1920s. Both these regions of Southern Manitoba are conservative, religious, agricultural, and economically centred around a larger town of about ten thousand souls. In other words, outsiders might look at these two places and think, *These are all the same people.*

Those outsiders would, largely, be right. Yet, within these two regions themselves, less so. Fun fact: there are these gentle, joshing Low German terms for one region to refer to the other, *Dit Sied* and *Jant Sied,* loosely translated to "This side" and "That over there side," referring to the west and east banks of the Red River, which splits the larger area of the province.

But joshing aside, my uncle was serious, decades after moving: "I still don't feel like I'm *from* there."

And a decade after I left, my old friend: "It's cool, he's from here."

What Community?

I BEGAN TO conceive this essay after rereading a magazine interview I'd done months prior. The interview was about my then new book of short stories *A Dream of a Woman*, and the interviewer had asked me about community. I'm a trans woman, and specifically the interviewer asked about community among trans people, or "the trans community." I echoed to him something a character says in the book: "that term 'the trans community' can mean whatever I want it to mean in that moment."[1]

The character in question does believe this whole-heartedly. But when I read back those words of mine, speaking for myself as a real-life human, I wondered if I was actually quite that cynical. The magazine had landed on my doorstep in the humidity of summer 2021, in a newly vaccinated Windsor, Ontario, gingerly waking from COVID quarantine. I knew I benefited from community. I was actively reconnecting with community! And Lord knows, I had dearly come to understand how I *needed* community during the bleak lockdown days.

Yet, I was still frustrated with the concept of community, as I had been most of my life. The drama, the groupthink, the way it turns against individuals it does not understand. Its problems felt intractable, replete with all too human Ouroboros and Gordian knots. I found myself still loath to examine "community" head-on, whether it be in the context of Mennonitism, a small city like Windsor, the neighbourhoods of New York City where I was newly spending the academic year, the Manitoba towns of my childhood, the Pacific Northwest suburbs of my adolescence, or the squabbling, interlaced array of queer communities in which I'd spent much of my adult life.[*]

Community. Just the word itself is so damn amorphous. It can describe everything from a Rust Belt city's literary scene to a network of Christian denominations to transsexuals bitching about electrolysis pain on the internet to unwieldy political blocs of racialized minorities to internet fandoms to organized hate groups to any homosexual-adjacent person who self-describes with the word *gay.* Somewhere along the line, such amorphousness had even caused the word *community* to attain semantic satiation for me—the phenomenon in which a word is repeated so often it loses its meaning; it ceases to sound like a word.

And when I really started thinking about this, I saw that term *community* invoked everywhere, in a manner at once authoritative and nebulous, a word that can, indeed, seemingly mean whatever its speaker wants.

Like, okay, look at influential forces like politicians, or multinational conglomerates, or even just the media. Netflix advertises the documentary *Disclosure:* "Leading trans creatives and thinkers share heartfelt perspectives and analysis about Hollywood's impact on the trans com-

....

[*] To wit: it's probably indicative that many queer people to whom I mentioned this essay's concept reacted with some combo of apprehension, shock, sympathy, and sometimes a deadpan why-are-you-doing-that-to-yourself.

munity."[2] The New York governor says of Black History Month: "A time for all New Yorkers to reflect on the many contributions of the Black community and the ongoing struggle for equality."[3] I can get off an airplane in Toronto and a bank advertisement on the jet bridge will proclaim the colonial nation-state of Canada "a close-knit community of 36 million." I can cancel my free Adobe trial and, after alarmingly clingy screens plead for me to reconsider, the confirmation screen arrives: "Casey, you're still part of the Adobe community."

On the tenth anniversary of the Deferred Action for Childhood Arrivals program,* an ABC affiliate reports: "The undocumented community says its future will remain uncertain until there's a clear pathway to citizenship."[4] The US president signs a bill related to gay marriage and praises the then Speaker of the House at the ceremony: "Equality and dignity for the LGBT community has always been her North Star."[5] A *Politico* article on a US Senate race: "Herschel Walker rallied with the Indian American community in September . . ."[6] A *Wall Street Journal* deck† on the backlash to a comedian's jokes: "the company faced strong criticism from the transgender community . . ."[7]

So here we have powerful entities referring to vast, disparate groups of far-flung people and doing so with a mien of authority, with the assumption that when they say "community," their audience understands what they mean, that nobody's going to ask for clarification. These powerful entities are also the type whose utterances are

....

* Also known as DACA, the program conferring some legal protections for some undocumented people in the US.

† Journalism-speak for the small headline running below a main headline in a news article

usually subject to multiple rounds of review as well as quick public criticism—in other words, if a term would be confusing or get them in trouble, they might not use it. But "community" is invoked without question all the time.

I believe in community. I believe in its necessity. I believe it is deeply and irrevocably meaningful to humanity and to our individual lives. And yet: What do these powerful entities *mean?*

Take the phrase "the [X] community." When I read that phrase, I think: *How does this person know this about the [X] community? What are the borders of the [X] community? How is the writer deciding who counts within them and who does not? Is the writer a member of the [X] community? Would others dispute their membership? Whatever claim is made about the community, how many sections within it must the claim apply to in order to justify the term?* Perhaps most importantly, *How can that writer possibly decide who gets to speak for the community? And who are those not speaking in their place?*

Now, as a writer, I get it. More specific phrasing than "the [X] community" can get prolix, and the pressure of word economy closes in. Still, my bullshit radar pings.

Take the last of the examples above, "the transgender community." How would, say, that writer at the *Wall Street Journal* define it, if pressed? How would *I* define it if pressed? Certainly, if you asked me off the street, I doubt I'd come up with much beyond: "Goodness, that's complicated. I don't know."

* * *

HERE, WITH THE luxury of slow consideration, both thinking on aspirational wide-tent definitions *and* capturing
how the term actually gets functionally used, let me take
some stabs at possible definitions of "the transgender
community."

The transgender community is:

- anyone whose sex or gender differs from that
  assigned at birth. Put another way, the trans community is all trans people.
- anyone who explicitly identifies as transgender. Difficult to measure numbers, but the Williams Institute
  pegs it as roughly 1 in 200 adults in the US,[8] which
  scans as reasonable to me.
- any trans person in relations with other trans people:
  friends, lovers, spouses, co-workers, organizers, et al.
  (A phrase I hear often is *being in community with* others, using *community* as a verb. I'll return to this.)
- anyone active in trans politics, social services, culture, and other work incorporating the considerations
  and needs of trans people.
- the trans people most visible and palatable to main-
  stream media and society, and thus accordingly some
  mixture of cis-passing, skinny, white, college-edu-
  cated, and already famous/notable before they
  transitioned.
- whichever trans activists are the loudest and most
  uncompromising voices in the room on a given issue.
- any group of trans people whom a given transgender
  person feels like bitching about that day.
- any group of trans people whom a given cisgender
  journalist feels like bitching about that day.
- all trans people plus some cis people who, say, are

active in trans movements or perhaps parent trans
children or are partners of trans people.

- all trans people plus those who don't identify as trans
now but likely well might someday—such as those
unable to come out or who are actively questioning
or who are simply unaware of certain language or
options. Example: when I was sixteen, I explicitly
said and believed that I was not transgender, because
back then I had a different idea of what that meant
than I do now, even though I was running around in
skirts and painting my nails and posting on my Live-
Journal about "wanting to be a girl."

- whatever a given trans person wants it to be when
they invoke it.

- all these stuck-up bitches who just don't fucking understand what it means to be part of a community . . .

Okay, I'll cut it off there. All these statements have
their problems—even the more innocuous ones. Saying
"the transgender community is all trans people," for
example, doesn't always hold water. Many trans people do
not like the specific word *transgender* and prefer a different term (including me, actually!*) and many trans people

----

* Unpacking time: In my day-to-day life, among friends, I refer to myself as a
transsexual—I just like the word better, and I like how it reflects my specific
experience, that of a woman who was raised as a boy, a social and corporeal
experience that feels closer to *sex* to me than *gender,* even though it's a bit
semantic. I don't particularly *mind* the term *transgender* and I'm happy to be
included within its umbrella, but when I use that term, it's more out of polit-
ical/social lubrication and convenience than anything. There were once,
however, intense intra-community debates over using the terms and delineating their differences! Both *transgender* versus *transsexual* as well as
transvestite. I find these days saying *trans* has functionally papered over much
of these differences, and continues to do so, but there are also alternatives
that don't even use the prefix *trans* at all—*gender-variant,* for example. To wit:
this is just some of what whirs through my head when I see anybody (cis and

will tell you they don't *feel* a part of "the trans community" or do not want to be, and in any case don't consider themselves in it. Plus, any non-subjective definition of *trans people* is impossible to pin down. An intersex person, for example, might not consider themselves trans even as they consider themselves someone "whose sex or gender differs from that assigned at birth."

Context matters enormously. Sometimes this is self-evident. For example, invoking "the transgender community" will bring to mind different entities when discussing regimens of hormone therapy than it will on Jayne County's contributions to punk music or the heartbreaking current political backlash against trans rights in the US and UK. But even issues that seem cause for cohesion in a community can provoke disparate forces, and not always in the way you'd guess. A personal memory: When Caitlyn Jenner began praising Donald Trump in 2016,[9] I guessed most trans people who disliked Trump* would disdain this action. And plenty of trans people did just that and exhibited shock and outrage. But plenty of us also did not care or expected behaviour like this from Jenner, or could not be interested in expending emotional energy on the subject. And I did not necessarily find these variant reactions to map cleanly onto an individual's temperament or where their specific politics fit.

This unpredictability is boring old human nature, of course, and an extension of the fact that our emotional "*This is terrible!*" responses tend to be heterogeneous and disorderly. As Theda Hammel says, you pick what you get

trans) breeze through the term *the transgender community* within a sentence.

* Which is the vast majority of US trans people, but that's a different subject.

mad about.[10] But that's just it: When someone invokes "the trans community," as in the above "the [X] community" examples, I just think, how can *anyone* blithely use that term without qualification? When I hear that phrase, I wonder if what they actually mean, whether they know it or not, is "a few trans people I am aware of."

Now, often this term is invoked by harried, over-worked people trying their best, especially with regards to journalists. I don't suspect malice or a conspiracy as the culprit here (not usually, anyway*). Still, when they use the term *the trans community*, I believe they are simplifying something to the point of untruth.

. . . I almost ended this chapter by saying "this term *the trans community* doesn't *mean* anything to me anymore."

But if I'm honest with myself, that's not true either.

When, say, Netflix invokes "the trans community," my brain envisions a fundamentally different image than when my friends say "the trans community." I'll try to explain: When Netflix says it, I see a scatterplot of non-profit talking heads, media-friendly activists, and a selection of loud popular social media accounts on the internet. When my friends say it, I envision a mélange of mutual acquaintances and local circles, mixed with some accounts on social media but usually different from the Netflix-conjured ones, accounts with lower follower totals, those belonging to people my friends and I kinda know, but not personally.

---

* No pleasure in having to clarify this, but I do believe there are some malicious actors involved in coverage of trans issues from certain media organizations, ranging from legacy newspapers to conservative cable news to British tabloids. Not what I'm focusing on for the purposes of this conversation; this is about the people who are trying to get it right. But, that shit is real.

Both these visions are blurry, without firm boundaries, but they're largely distinct and they *are* immediate. What I think about when I hear the term depends entirely on the context and the standpoint of the speaker. I think if you're going to invoke "the [X] community," it probably demands an understanding that the term is inherently clunky, and at least one modifying adjective, perhaps several (sometimes the pressure of word economy has to deal!).

Like, for trans people, given that we are everywhere on the planet and are usually divided by geography, race, and class—important examples yet just three among a near-infinite number of factors—if I hear the term *the trans community* without any further clarifying context, it's impossibly abstract to *me*, even as tiny and specific a group as we are. (An analogy: Think of how nonsensically general a phrase like "the Idaho community" would sound in the context of discussing US life. Statistically speaking, Idahoans are also 1 in 200 people in the country.)

One economical solution I use in my own personal life is the phrase *my [X] communities*. To say "my trans communities" or "my writer communities" implies something more accurate and specific yet leaves room for heterogeneity. There's an understanding of internal range built into it. It's subtle and imperfect, but it's a meaningful difference.

Moving back to the examples above: as a reader or listener, when I hear a phrase like *the [X] community,* I try to ask myself, *What does* [X] community *mean to me? What does it mean to the speaker? And what can I learn from the differences?*

For me, this particularly goes for communities I'm *not* part of. Example: I'm white, and when a journalist refers to, say, "the undocumented community" without further context, I can only think: *Do they know what they're talking about? Do I? Even if I don't, should I accept how they use this term?*

And even when all these pains are taken, humility should be consistently summoned, the recognition of unknown unknowns kept steady. Assumptions are as instant and human as farts, and repressing them is folly, but. Recognize them for what they are. Noor Naga has a passage in her novel *If an Egyptian Cannot Speak English:* "Those outside of a language, a culture, see furniture through a window and believe it is a room. But those inside know there are infinite rooms just out of view, and that they can always be more deeply inside."[11]

Assumptions (2)

MY MOTHER HAS always been invested in knowing her neighbours. Back in our small town in the Pembina Valley, we knew everyone on the block, and the retired couple on the other side of our duplex often looked after me when my mom was at work. When my school insisted we sell, like, chocolate almonds or something, I would run around the neighbourhood by myself, alone, carrying my dinky little box, and people recognized me as my mom's kid and invited me in and no one questioned that I was running around on my own, everyone assumed it was okay. (Also, I sold lots of chocolate, no big deal.)

When we left, it was to a suburban area of the Pacific Northwest. Those neighbourly relations of hers became ... more difficult. First we landed in a sprawling apartment community; we lived in a rowhouse-like structure next to three other families. My mom knocked on everyone's door to introduce us, and she had come up with a great idea: What if we had a pot luck with each course of the meal at a different house? Appetizers at the first house, salad at the second house, main course at the third house, dessert at the last house? It didn't catch on. She really tried. One family was blank-faced at the very idea; they seemed confused at my mother's outreach, her friendliness, her assumption they might want to participate.

Later, we moved across town to the house where I'd live until leaving home, at the end of a cul-de-sac on the north edge of town, a neat picture of bedroom-community upward mobility. My mother tried again. She, I, and my stepdad marched up to every house on the block offering food: "Hello, we're your new neighbours!" But no one wanted to be friends. I never went inside a single person's home in the five years I lived there.

Much later, my mother spoke of this with a tinge of sadness. "If I had to do it again, I probably wouldn't live on this block." It was then I realized, latently, that she and my stepdad both grew up in truly small towns of maybe a couple hundred people, more villages than towns really. And all Mennonites like them. The idea of not knowing your neighbours was as ludicrous as not knowing the family in your own house. "I probably wouldn't live on this block." An interesting choice of words. I wonder if it would have been different one or two blocks over.

Unbifurcation

THERE'S A DRIER, simpler usage of *community*, of course. It's the other way you can read it in a news article, like this: "Dr Becher grew up in Sissonville, a small community an hour west of Clay."[12]

In this context, *community* means a fixed space that can be precisely and quantitatively measured. There are firm, material contours involved; if you live within the town limits of Sissonville, West Virginia, then you are one of the 4,084 people in that community. I could apply this definition, say, to my childhood hometown in the Pembina Valley (current population: 9,929).

While brainstorming this essay, I was tempted to bifurcate the term *community*, delineating between these clearly enumerated varieties and those of the slipperier kind, these refracting intangibilities of *belonging* ("It's cool, he's from here," "I still don't feel like I'm *from* there"). It would've been my intent to focus on these latter kinds, as in the fascinating contradictions of defining something like *the trans community*.

But I soon realized, no, that was still too simple, that both tangible and intangible definitions of *community* will always collapse into each other eventually, neither quite able to stand long-term without its twin.

There's this book called *Harlem Is Nowhere: A Journey to the Mecca of Black America* by Sharifa Rhodes-Pitts, who wrote it after living in the famous Manhattan neighbourhood for nearly a decade. It's a dreamy, beautiful book. A review of it by Mark Reynolds begins thus:

Actually, there are two Harlems. There is, of course, the Harlem on the ground: the Manhattan neighborhood of roughly 3,900 [sic] square feet and almost a quarter of a million residents, the vast majority of whom are black. This Harlem is home to vexing urban storylines in microcosm, economic re-development and the future of public education, to name just two. It's also home to an awful lot of poverty, even amidst the refurbished brownstones and middle-to-upper-income residents. But mostly, the Harlem on the ground is the one where people live, breathe, eat, drink, struggle, rejoice and wake up the next day to do it all over again.

And there's the Harlem most people conjure when they hear the word, "Harlem." That's the one of opulence bathed in sepia, of magnificent churches and showplaces, of blackness' best and brightest. It's the Harlem in all those historic photos, spanning back close to a century, of black people living life at its fullest. Those images represented for the world the aspirations of a far-flung nation of millions, for whom Harlem was less a place than a state of mind, a destination less geographic than mythic.[13]

Reynolds's delineation here of what *Harlem* means to many Black people (I almost just wrote "the Black community"—it's so easy to do!) makes me wonder about all communities' mixing elements of on-the-ground facts and mythos. Even those that seem on their face to have little of the latter. To speak of, say, a Podunk small town and scoff, "That place is in the middle of fuckin' nowhere," is still, borrowing Reynolds's description, to form a *conjuring* of what a place means, to form a kind of mythological statement about it.

Indeed, the 1948 Ralph Ellison essay from which Rhodes-Pitts gets her title plays with this very concept. In writing of Black Americans' second-class status in the country, Ellison said: "In Harlem the reply to the greeting, 'How are you?' is often, 'Oh, man, I'm *nowhere*'."[14] And a friend of mine once described her hometown of Phoenix, with which her experiences were not good, as: "It's like God took a shit in the middle of the desert and two million people decided to move there." A conjuring to describe vacuousness is still a conjuring, a mythos of negation still a mythos. Think of Shelbyville in *The Simpsons*, or the small-town sitcom *Corner Gas*, in which the protagonists frequently invoke a neighbouring burg called Wullerton, and when they do so, everyone in earshot spits on the ground. The camera almost never actually *shows* Wullerton itself, yet the meaning of the place is clear.

Or, rather, *a* meaning, according to these specific characters. I don't mean to dwell on vacuousness. The cascading possible multiplicities of these meanings and mythos is also part of how communities function. Rhodes-Pitts writes of a teenage awakening to these multiplicities in her youth in Texas, viewing destitute photos of Depression-era Harlem and contrasting them with her romantic knowledge of the Harlem Renaissance: "I did not understand how this place existed as both haven and ghetto ... It also revealed something damning about the history I had learned—*a flattened version of events where a place is allowed to be only one thing or the other*."[15] (emphasis mine)

Benedict Anderson, writing in 1982 on the idea of nations, opined that a country was an "imagined political community ... imagined because the members of even the smallest nation will never know most of their fellow-members, meet them, or even hear of them, yet in the minds of each lives the image of their communion."[16] He goes on: "An American will never meet, or even know the names of more than a handful of his 240,000,000-odd fellow Americans. He has no idea of what they are up to at any one time. But he has complete confidence in their steady, anonymous, simultaneous activity."[17]

Even in the small town of my childhood—a quaint picture of a tiny community that would be considered a dust speck on a map by many—well, thousands of people are still *thousands*. You can't know everyone! The element of imagination and mystery is more obvious in a big place, but it also remains inherent in a small one.* Even a small place is never just one thing or the other. Multiplicities

....

* Such imaginations and mysteries also including what counts as "big" or "small." I went to high school in Eugene, Oregon, a city of about 140,000 at the time. When we moved there, we regarded it as much bigger than we did when we left. I have certain memories of arriving there that centre my mother being so excited to be around culture that our Mennonite prairie towns could not offer—big bookstores, a university. And then, fifteen years later, when she moved up to the Portland area, she referred to Eugene as a small town too, even as she had grown up in her literal village, and knew what the smallest possible towns looked like.

of meaning fracture down to every level. Rhodes-Pitts writes frequently of her particular block in *Harlem Is Nowhere,* and after recounting a story about an elderly neighbour's childhood, she says:

> There are other stories I have forgotten because I didn't write them down, and if I lived on a different block I would be told different stories. This fact strikes me when passing a corner that is not my own, where, in front of the liquor store or the bodega there stand arrayed a group of men—strangers to me, but familiar in disposition. They warily eye my advance until I broach a hello, inviting a chorus of returned salutations. If I tarried a bit longer, or invented a reason to pass those other spots with regularity, I might gain a new set of friends and a new set of stories ... But I say hello and continue, thinking to mind my own business ... knowing that I could never linger long enough on enough different corners to hear all that everyone had to say.[18]

(Makes me wonder about my mother again. "If I had to do it again, I probably wouldn't live on this block.")

To turn it back to the impossibility of bifurcation—these multiplicities of meaning exist not only within a community's imaginary mythos but also in its firm, material contours. Example: A place like Sissonville, West Virginia, is certainly a "small community," as the newspaper says. It has clear borders marked out by the county, and the 2020 census enumerates 4,084 people as living there.[19] Now, for one, that fact became inaccurate the second the census closed up shop and someone moved either in or out, but more significantly, what can those material contours capture of a person who lives a few minutes outside the town limits but works, dates, and socializes within them?

Or perhaps consider the New York City neighbourhood of Marble Hill, which today is part of the borough of Manhattan but on a map looks undeniably part of the Bronx, the neighbouring borough to the north. What gives? In the 1890s, a canal was dug on the neighbourhood's south end, which made it into an island and separated it from Manhattan's land mass, and then decades later the river was filled in on its *north* side, in the end linking it physically with the Bronx and the US mainland, and this all created a confusion so persistent that a man who went on to represent the neighbourhood on city council was unaware which borough it actually belonged to until he began campaigning.[20]

Or consider the requirements of "proof of address," necessary to access certain institutional services, a demand many can meet with a simple utility bill or driver's licence, but also many cannot. What happens to their enumeration?

Or what of my grandfather, who technically lived an hour outside his home community of Blumenort, Manitoba, all through the 1990s in the aftermath of marital turmoil, but who visited every weekend to tend the garden of the house he still owned and where his wife from whom he was separated still lived; he visited to clear the eaves, to mow the lawn, to play with his grandchildren and sleep in the spare room while his wife lay alone in their marital bed on the other side of the wall. My grandfather, who was sixty years old, and to whom this essay is dedicated (rest in peace), would lie in that single bed on blue-white linoleum floors in the village where he'd lived for half a century, since he was just a boy, inside a room where decades ago his now-grown children had once all slept.

I am trying to lay out as baseline fact that no community can be completely mapped or pinned down, that no community can escape an element of imagination and mystery—not in the mythological sense, like "opulence bathed in sepia," and also not in its plainest forms, like "Current population: 9,929."

A Small Working List of Synonyms for Community

Population
Village
Neighbourhood
Scene
Fellowship
Kinship
Town
Block
Circle
Clique
Society
Nation
World
Gang
Public
Culture
Subculture
District
People
A Few People I Am Aware Of

Assumptions (3)

FOR A FEW years, I worked as a book publicist for Biblio-asis, a small independent literary press and the publishers of this very essay. This was also in Windsor—a Rust Belt town of a quarter million nestled in the southern crook of Canada, across the border from Detroit.

One day at the office, in the late afternoon, I got a text from a girl I'd met in Iowa through a couple I was friends with. They had given her my number. The girl said she was in Windsor and she was stranded. She'd been on a bus to Toronto but had trouble at customs, and the bus left by the time they let her through. She had no place to go. Could she ... ?

"Yes, of course you can crash!" I said. I gave my three housemates a heads-up, and they all confirmed: yes, of course she could crash. She bused over before I was off work. My housemates, who did not know her, let her in. They showed her the spare room. I drove home and we all hung out and drank red wine and talked till late. And she slept the night in our house and took off again on the bus to Toronto the next day.

None of this was fraught or difficult, it was all instantly convivial. She was already chatting warmly with my housemates when I walked in. Even I barely knew her, we had met only once in Iowa, and it was in a social atmosphere and not for that long. But this still all happened calmly, without question.

Every one of the seven people involved in the above story is a transsexual. We all made assumptions and they were the correct ones.

The next day at work, after the girl left, I wondered about my cis co-workers. How translatable my experience might be to them, how they might find themselves in similar scenarios, and how they might not. I kept thinking about it. My co-workers were considerate, generous people, the kind who would absolutely put up a friend of a friend in need. But I did feel a separation between me and them. I felt it.

Years later, looking back, I'm not sure why I did. After all, it's a pretty common experience to put up your friends travelling through town. Particularly in communal living situations, one might find oneself playing host to a stranger, as my housemates did. There's nothing uniquely trans about that. Further, all seven people in the above story are a bunch of other things: all white, all went to college for at least a bit, all artsy weirdos who can bond about artsy weirdo stuff.

Did transness really lubricate this interaction of putting up my friend? I do think so, yes. Was the separation I felt between my co-workers and me that morning a good thing? Probably not, but I felt it. I wonder a lot about the presence/absence of friction in these kinds of situations, what lubricates help and hospitality, and what doesn't.

* * *

YOU CAN'T TAKE buses from Windsor to Toronto anymore, though. Not as I'm writing this, anyway, in the spring of 2022. Greyhound shut down across all of Canada. It was a long time coming; the routes out west from my childhood that connected our communities have all been closed for years.

When I was a kid, the bus is how I travelled to Winnipeg to see my dad on weekends. My mom was regularly busy at work and my dad didn't have a car. Recently, I asked my cousin how people get there and back if they don't have wheels. She said everyone does rideshares. Part of me was charmed by that. Part of me was a bit sad. It is kind of nice to see an organic community response to fill such an essential service; it's reminiscent of something like cork bulletin boards in cafés and grocery stores as a way to anonymously trade availability and need. And also, well, there's a lot of people out there who used the bus in those rural areas[21]—seniors without cars, members of remote Indigenous communities,[22] women fleeing bad domestic situations, people who didn't have money but maybe had time, people who were all those things at once. Seems an unbenevolent rupture to be at the mercy of whoever happens to be doing a rideshare that weekend.

For my mother, if she was in the same situation now as she was back then, I doubt she could've located trusted, dependable humans with whom to send out her seven-year-old kid on Manitoba winter highways. Though perhaps that's unfair. Maybe we would've adjusted and found a way. Maybe.

Verbs

"COMMUNITY IS A verb." I see this phrase all the time. It's the name of a podcast. It's the name of an NPR *Notes from America* episode. Searching it on social media gets you a big tranche of hits.[23] [24] Vancouver activist Gabrielle Peters said it when she organized pizzas to be delivered to local warming shelters one night when temps abnormally plunged to twenty degrees below zero, warming shelters she knew would be packed and not have food.[25]

It's an idea I appreciate, that community is not a thing but a motion. Sometimes it's natural and boring, and sometimes it takes effort and work, but: it only assumes shape via activity.

Hence also why I like that phrase "being in community with." I tend to use that in my everyday life. I like the active-ness of it. I like how completing the phrase pushes one slightly towards specificity, and away from the abstract-ness of "the [X] community." It also kinda invokes the idea of communion, in both the non-religious and the religious sense.

Thinking of *community* as a verb also gives it more weight as a dynamic and shifting force, more akin to river than tree.

* * *

SOMETIMES, COMMUNITY IS a motion that is both natural and boring *and* takes effort and work. (I am continuously fascinated by this duality whenever it crops up.)

In my late twenties, I attended a small Mennonite church. We met in a bland one-storey building that used to be a laundromat. It looked very un-church-like, though there's a tradition of plain, unadorned church structures in Mennonite communities. At the time, I'd never attended services regularly as an adult. But I wanted to go.

One day, an elderly couple in the church needed help at home. They didn't attend regularly anymore, I'd never met them; by the time I showed up, they were having trouble getting out of the house. Their adult daughter wasn't around that week. I volunteered to help. I drove to a building I'd never visited, travelled up an elevator, took their basket of laundry, and washed the underwear of this old couple whom I'd never before spoken to, and never would again. And I thought nothing of it. It took effort and work out of my day to do this, and it was also natural and boring.

I'm not telling you this to showcase piety or whatever. I'm telling you this because I was familiar with the particular churches of my childhood, and an unspoken thing from them still lived in my body: when someone else in the church needs help, you help. Even if you barely know them. It was the kind of thing I understood as something you just *do*. *Community* as a verb, something simple and quiet.

NOW, I DON'T mean to be so rosy. There are flip sides to all this. With this couple . . . like I said, I never saw them again, I don't know what happened to them. (More river than tree indeed.) And I didn't attend that church for long—the pastor I loved left suddenly one day, and I couldn't deal and stopped going for a bit and then inertia set in. Leaving intractable questions of religion aside, what does that say? About effort and work regarding community? I want to talk about all this.

Community is a verb. Verbs are actions, actions are limited. I believe in the phrase "*Community* is a verb," and I'm glad it's so popular. I'm also a little wary about the oft-under-bubbling implication alongside that community is a panacea.

Peters addressed that too with her pizza drive, though her comments in this respect got less media attention. In one CTV article, the lead quotes from her are brazenly of the Live-Laugh-Love variety: "Nobody is going to save us but us," and "We have to be there to care for each other." There's necessary truth in those platitudes, of course. But in the article's penultimate paragraph was also this: "[Peters's] real hope is that the government steps up and provides more—more food, more shelters, more housing."

Among the many problems with abstracting "community" are the vastly divergent material realities across communities! To this end, I don't think it's a coincidence that Peters is also a disability activist. Some communities have fewer resources than others, and saying, "We have to take care of ourselves," well, that assumes the care in question is a resource available to be given, no? I dunno. I don't want to get into the weighty questions of how and whether the state should solve these problems, but. Even as community is immensely powerful, it also can't always save us all, and I think it's dangerous for rhetoric to imply otherwise. Power and privilege restrict some communities more than others, just like anything else.

Sometimes I've seen "Community is everything" gush across my social media. It's not true. Community is an action; actions have limits.

The Power of the Group

WE ARE DRAWN to certain narratives—we *choose* certain narratives to believe. I think of the narratives we choose to pass on, and those we don't want to look at.

My father went to high school in Edmonton, Alberta, in the 1970s, and he got the lead part in a production of *Godspell*. This other guy, he really wanted the part, this aspirational actor with formal training and dreams of being a professional. But my dad, having grown up in the Mennonite church, knew something deeper about the religious material.

So: My dad gets the role. And this other guy, he never gets over it. After the show closes, at the cast party, the guy comes up to my dad and goes off about how he's a better actor, he could've played the part much better, blah blah blah, and kinda works himself into a rage! Eventually, he hits my dad in the face. To which my dad simply says: "If your enemy strikes you on your right cheek, offer him your left."

He hits my dad again.

My dad says, "Had enough?"

And the other guy puts down his hands and starts crying.

... That's the story my dad *told* me, at least.

He's also the person who taught me that old saying, "Never let the truth get in the way of a good story."

Today, as an adult, I can reflect on the fact that my father grew up in a violent household and a violent world, facts I've known since I was a child. (Mennonite ideology espouses pacifism. When it comes to individual Mennonites, well, let's just say it varies.) My dad is someone who, as a rule, wouldn't habitually respond to a strike on the face by turning the other cheek. And I think he'd freely admit that, too. My father has plenty of stories that involve anger and violence. But he had a narrative he wanted to impress on me when I was younger. Specifically, he wanted to break a cycle of violence when I came along. And he did it and I'll love him forever because of it, and that story about *Godspell* was part of it.

And: I don't know if it all happened the way he described it. Of course I don't. Maybe it did, but for such purposes, it didn't really matter. He had a narrative and he wanted it to do something and it worked.

Another story. My friend Stephen once worked as a care aide for adults in group living. Sometimes he accompanied clients into town, to shop or hang out or whatever. They'd often go to thrift stores.

One day, they go into the thrift store run by the Mennonite Central Committee. And his client starts freaking out, which isn't uncommon—he starts screaming and shrieking in the middle of the store. Stephen told me that whenever this happened in public, invariably they were asked to leave. But, in this case, the old Mennonite woman minding the store does not ask them to leave. All she does is sidle up to Stephen, nod stoically at his client, and say, "He's upset."

Those are two warm stories about my people. I love to tell them when I'm feeling fond. Here's a third story. In my mid-twenties, I worked in a café in Winnipeg. And one night one of the regulars, an old handyman originally from Western Manitoba, he finds out I'm of Mennonite extraction. He tells me what he said people knew back home: That when a Mennonite man ran into trouble with the law—particularly in domestic matters, say he was known to be violent with his wife—and when the police attempted to intervene, the elders would say, "We'll handle it in the church." And the police let them. That was the phrase: "We'll handle it in the church." So, this old handyman tells me, "When Mr Penner or Mr Friesen* got into a scrape, they'd handle it in the church." And the cops left them alone. When Miriam Toews's novel *Women Talking* came out a few years later, based on a real-life Bolivian Mennonite group whose male leaders systematically sheltered the mass rape of their colony's women and girls—I heard the echo of the old handyman. *We'll handle it in the church.*

The first two stories above are about individuals, but this one is more about community. This is community functioning how it's intended, protecting its people—a certain male demographic within it, anyway. (And outside the community, well ... the Mennonites of that area are virtually all white, and in the rest of the province of Manitoba there are many populations the cops do not

----

* Friesen and Penner are common Russian Mennonite last names.

leave alone.) *Community* is a verb, communities have power, and power can service the ends it likes.

All three of these stories were told to me as personal anecdote, and told to me a certain way, and I am choosing to believe they are all true. I do believe they're true. It is also an active choice I am making.

Sofia Samatar has a section in her futuristic short story "Fallow" where the protagonist Agar makes a historical presentation to a group of Mennonites. She wants to talk about sordid episodes of their past. It doesn't go well. "This episode in our history was a wound," says Agar; "the cells of the body sprang into action when it was touched, closing about it, closing it down." In another scene, Agar writes of a kind teacher who agitates the community and later dies by suicide. "I understood then that she had a horror of the exercise of power, not only the obvious sorts of power—the rod, the shout—but the type we knew most intimately: The power of the group. She had a horror of the downcast eye that waits for others to act."[26] In that scene, the classroom has grown rowdy and begun to form against her, and the teacher's instinct is to know that the group will always win.

The power of the group. This is getting into the dark side of these thoughts of community. If a cohesive, strong community is akin to a body, you can always find dark, bleak veins pumping blood throughout it. If it is akin to a river, a strong current powered by many natural streams, then it will, from time to time, contain something that gets you sick. My personal experiences have taught me this is more rule than exception.

In a trans arts gathering I was once part of, one of the organizers was accused of abuse from another trans woman she'd dated. The organizer's presence continued in the gathering while she participated in an accountability process, attempting to work through and repair the harm. This process fixed little.

Many activist/leftist groups attempt these accountability processes, often with the language of what's known as *restorative justice*—attempting to find alternatives to police and punishment, focusing both on rehabilitating the offender and healing the victim. I share these ideals; I am not a pro-police person, I do not want to solve community conflict via the cops, and I have heard of accountability processes that turned out well. And yet. Still. I think of the above trans arts gathering, and the ensuing shambles that resulted from our attempt to deal with it, and I think of that social justice–focused language of accountability processes, and I hear the old handyman from Western Manitoba: *We'll handle it in the church.*

I bring this all up to serve not nihilism but a hopefully productive cynicism. I think we should keep in steady rotation a certain recurring question: What within a community do its members not want to look at? What gets one starry-eyed? What does that starry-eyed-ness prevent one from seeing clearly? *What narratives about my communities, no matter how I feel about them that day, are true that I do not want to hear?*

Kai Cheng Thom, for example, observed a laudable emphasis on *safety* in her social justice left circles. She also observed that the queer community centres she'd worked at would "restrict the access of mentally ill trans women and homeless people because their very presence makes middle-class queers feel 'unsafe.'"[27] A true thing we perhaps don't want to hear; such is the hard stuff of these questions. (A friend once said on this topic: "We don't have the right to *feel* safe, we have the right to actually *be* safe.")

There is potential for dark action in any group no matter how good of intention or heart. The possibility is always there. I really believe that. The fiction writer Rawi Hage once wrote, "Over time, I had learned that the strength of a close-knit social group lies in its ability to compartmentalize."[28] Some stories you love to tell and some you don't. Cells of the body spring into action around a wound, closing about it, closing it down.

God

PERHAPS THERE IS a spectre that can haunt a people—the spectre of community. I cannot count how many times I've heard the worry about getting "blacklisted" or "cancelled" by "the community," in a way that *individually* often seems outsized and melodramatic, yet taken *collectively* is so common. Relatedly, one of few things seemingly uniting every politician in all the places I've lived, across party, race, geography, and country, is making repeated paeans to "the community," paeans that have such polish I hear a tinge of . . . desperation. A reader of this essay relayed a friend's observation of how "community" is invoked in Homoland: "It's like we think the community is GOD."

Coming from a Mennonite background, being intimately acquainted with the fear of godly retribution, of an ever-present force both watching you and ready to *punish*—the spiritual similarity of this observation is a little too close for my comfort.[*] Towards my friends, I always

....

[*] And indeed in some circles this is explicit theology! My own forebears believed deeply in its importance, that through community lay part of the divine. "So in Christ we, though many, form one body, and each member belongs to all the others." (Romans 12:4–5)

want to say something like: *No one is thinking about cancelling you! No one cares that much!* And yet, regardless of whether that's true or not, what does it say that the fear is so persistent? As Kristin Dombek wrote, "Any monster that feels so real must speak to us somehow."*

Part of me wants to fault abstraction again here—thinking of "the community," a vague, dough-y force rising up to cancel you, probably feels scarier than if, say, you were forced to enumerate a dozen specific influential people within a certain community, and then consider whether and how they'd actually perform said cancelling. Another facet of the twinning of mythos and geography, maybe.

But I know too that confronting abstraction is simply the low-hanging fruit of facing this fear, this fear of the power of the group.

One night, many years ago, after a night of commiserating with friends about a girl I'll call A, I decided to terminate my friendship with her, and I did it with righteous cruelty—I emailed A and told her, verbatim, that she'd hurt everyone I'd ever loved. Which at the time I believed. Which I had the proverbial receipts for, about which I could've told you in detail. This was two decades ago; whatever her supposed sins, I have forgotten the details, though I'm certain it was garden-variety high school drama.

What I *do* remember is how strongly I felt, when I cast out my friend, that I was doing the right thing. I felt

---

* From her book *The Selfishness of Others: An Essay on the Fear of Narcissism*, which I footnote here to hat-tip its brilliance and to thank its author, who shared space with me at a residency and once mailed me back a lost scarf after I left it in some cabin belonging to somebody I do not remember, I was drunk as hell, it was my last day at said residency, Kristin I love your writing so much and it helped me write this! Thank you for mailing my scarf back to my silly ass!

brave, writing A that email. Like I was standing up for the people I believed she'd hurt. And those people cheered me on. You might say I fancied myself standing up for my community. The power of the group. How real it is. A lesbian friend from a Mennonite family in one of those Manitoba villages confided in me once: When she came out, her parents supported her. Which ... was enough for her parents to not be too welcome around the church anymore. This had happened over a decade ago by the time we met, and things with her community had got better by then. But the pain and rage of the ostracization had stayed. How could it not? Incidentally, her village happens to be my other grandfather's hometown. Some of my extended family probably shunned hers.

The power of the group. Its punishment can leave a mark and keep people in line for a long time. Even if that punishment happens just once or twice. How real the fear of that power is. Even when it's just a prospect dangled in front of you. A spectre. (That party in my hometown: "Who the *fuck* is that?")

Needs

I WANT TO talk about all this. In doing so, let me clearly plant my stake in the ground: humans need community. Every piece of our knowledge tells us this. Isolation and loneliness are deadly, like *actually* deadly. It's hard to quantify such experiences, but researchers taking stabs posit that social isolation drags down a person's mortality as much as alcoholism or smoking.[29] "A 32% increased risk of stroke," particularly in people above fifty, says the CDC.[30] A Harvard study from the first year of COVID dispassionately reports, "Early mortality . . . depression, anxiety, heart disease, substance abuse, and domestic abuse"—these are, they say, "the potentially steep costs of loneliness."[31]

Heart disease? Stroke? A risk that rivals smoking and boozing?! As it turns out. As it turns out, loves. Being alone is bad for you—and it's not all about close family and friends. "Talking to strangers," says Robert Waldinger, who leads the longest-running study on human happiness, "actually makes us happier. There's good research on this."[32] (It's true, there's lots.[33]) Even in the initial terrifying days of the pandemic, where few were counselling against physical distancing, the NIH warned of drastic health consequences in the elderly brought on by "an acute, severe sense of social isolation and loneliness."[34] And on the other side of generations, the same for young people, among whom anxiety and depression in 2020 was at nearly *twice* the levels of the general population.[35] In *All About Love,* bell hooks wrote that we make communities "to ensure human survival everywhere in the world... communities sustain life—not nuclear families, or the 'couple,' and certainly not the rugged individualist... even individuals who are raised in nuclear families usually experience it as merely a small unit within a larger unit of extended kin."[36] And in that article on that Harvard research above, the one dispassionately reporting early mortality and heart disease? The deck for that article begins so simply, almost AI-like in its awkward irrefutability: "Robust social network is key to easing pain."

One might say: Okay, sure, loneliness is bad, duh. But is community really the skeleton key to solving it? My argument is not that community alone can nullify these ills. My argument is that community is a vital but oft-neglected sibling of those rarefied entities that keep one away from isolation and despair; it rests right up there with cherished friends, a partner who loves you, a family of some stripe who love you back, a passion or commitment that gives you juice through the days. Few of us enjoy all those things in this life (I currently don't). But some combo of them makes existence worth living (as it does mine). I want to argue for community's import alongside them.

I think that even the most private and introverted among us still benefit deeply from community connections; almost everyone knows what it's like to enter a space with other humans and feel warmth. And, in kind, know that warmth's absence. When I told my father I was writing this essay on community, he responded, "That's something I never got. I never found my tribe." There's an epic Lana del Rey video where during the outro she says: "*Every night I used to pray that I'd find my people.*"[37] Everyone has their own instant idea of what these statements mean.

Small

OKAY, AND LOOK, sometimes all this is small. Sometimes these communal connections occur in traces, happenstance, serendipity. Sometimes it doesn't *always* take work. (Activity isn't always labour.)

Digital spaces are often derided as leading to the breakdown of society,[38] but they too are conveyors of community. You can be alone in a room with no wish or ability to physically interact with other humans but still be someone who dips an electronic toe in the river of others. Even if you're just lurking and not participating. "You can almost feel normal," says a ghostly character in Emily Zhou's *Girlfriends*, about silently watching posts go by online. "Like you're a member of some chorus, no matter what's going on with you."[39] It can mean something. Sometimes it means ugly things, of course. But I'm not always sure we recognize the nourishing parts of these digital spaces. And truly, I think that's been the case for a long time.

There's an old comic strip that's always stuck with me. It's from *Bloom County*. 1988. In the first panel, two characters, Opus and Hodge-Podge, are talking in front of a television. Opus is flipping through channels, the remote control going *bink bink bink*. Opus says, "Cable TV."

In the second panel, he continues, "Ya know, in years past, one could watch Jack Benny at 8 p.m. every Saturday night and know you're sharing the same moment with nearly every other American."

In the third panel, there's no dialogue, just Opus pressing the remote. *Bink bink bink bink bink.*

The last panel finds Opus stumbling onto soft-core porn. (Hodge-Podge says, "S'pose we're sharing this with Carol Burnett?"[40])

It's those initial nostalgic comments I've always remembered, "one could watch Jack Benny at 8 p.m. every Saturday night and know you're sharing the same moment with nearly every other American," along with the image of Opus—a wistful, sensitive protagonist—wordlessly pressing the remote control. *Bink bink bink bink bink.* It's that underlying idea: that he used to watch the same show with the rest of the country on Saturdays at eight o'clock, and he got a tiny need met in doing so, but that's all gone now. In the strip, the setting is spare and darkly lit, as *Bloom County* often was when it went indoors. The television is outsized and looming in each frame, a reflection of the lonely, detached, then-modern world of the 1980s that its creator Berkeley Breathed clearly saw.

Today, in the 2020s, I think this strip tells us two stories. First, that indirectly connecting with others via mass media is not a unique invention of the digital age. And, second, that mourning the fraying of those connections, to regard the ongoing losses and shifts of mass media as *inherently isolating*—that's also an old story, with its own cycles of worry with each new development.

Now: I'm sympathetic to the position that the harms of social media are grim and real, in ways we probably

don't yet quite understand.[41] But I'm skeptical of easy culprits, and I'm skeptical of the oft-repeated idea[42] [43] that
today's digital world is marching us into an isolated
doom. (Further, some closer analysis suggests that, at
least before the pandemic, loneliness was not a problem
getting steadily worse or better.[44]) Social media, smart-
phones, desktop computers, Walkmans, cable TV, that
very same broadcast era with three channels that Opus
pines for—they were all blamed at one point as corrosive
to the community bonds of the time. A Toni Morrison
character in *Sula*—a novel spanning the 1910s to the
1960s—laments the invention of the telephone and that
new broadcast era of the television, because it meant
fewer people stopping by the house.[*] [45]

In reference to the strong social ties of nineteenth-
century, pre-urban America—those of the barn-raising
and midwifing rural variety—Robert Putnam wrote in
Bowling Alone: "Some early sociologists thought that this
thicket of informal social connection would not survive a
transplant into the anonymous city, that urbanization
would doom both friendship and extended kinship. However, experience showed that even in the most densely
populated urban settings, social filaments linking residents were steadily regenerated."[46] (A funny quote in
itself, as much of Putnam's book conversely exudes more
doomerist Opus-like hand-wringing.[†])

....

* The full quote is its own thing to consider: "These young ones kept talking
  about the community, but they left the hills to the poor, the old, the stub-
  born—and the rich white folks. Maybe it hadn't been a community, but it had
  been a place. Now there weren't any places left, just separate houses with
  separate televisions and separate telephones and less and less dropping by."
  The loss is real, is the loss not also age-old?

† Reading this book today, nearly a quarter century after its 2000 publication,
  illuminates the limits of the hard conclusions we can make about this stuff.

The concern about loss brought by progress is a continuing story, and I would suggest that, in a Janus-like fashion, that concern is usually both relevant and exaggerated. Like: Sure, it's complex, but are we maybe not always losing and gaining here? Because community can be fractured and slippery and seemingly ever at risk of dissolution at the same time that it can consistently regroup and resolder itself, mutate in ever-new fashions, form a balm to meet needs in ways it is difficult to predict or imagine.

I don't want to oversell this too much, particularly with social media—which, again, I don't think we quite understand what that's doing to us yet. Social trust is low in the United States. There's evidence that the potential for political organizing on social media, particularly Twitter, has had countervailingly stultifying effects.[47] Even if loneliness is not a progressively worsening problem, it's still an enormous ill no individual anecdote can paper over.[48]

And yet: for all the vats of ink spilled on these issues, I wonder if there aren't also seams of growing light we miss, steady heartbeats of communal well-being that still function. They deserve a bit of ink too.

To shift away from media of any variety: When I lived full-time in Windsor, I went through a breakup that took several years. Those weren't bad years, but it sometimes sucked, and I was often deeply sad, and I spent a lot of time in bars. I didn't really make friends in those bars. But I was enough of a regular in a few places that I soon

Some of the trends Putnam deplored have since spectacularly reversed—voting, for example—and some of the data he relied on don't quite feel like they bear the load he piles on them. He deplored the measurable decline in having people over for dinner and card games, for instance, but he also wrote in the era of the LAN party! Phenomena which would've been fascinating to examine, but which I wonder if he had any knowledge of, and which, of course, has also since bitten the technological dust.

consistently felt welcome and watched over, and to this day there are a handful of establishments where I will walk in and see a person I recognize and they will wave their hands and say, "How's it going, Casey?"*

I never got any of these folks' contacts and they never got mine. In retrospect, this suited me perfectly. They weren't strangers, but they weren't exactly friends. Often the word *acquaintances* is used to describe that kind of relationship, but they didn't feel like acquaintances, they felt like community. I think too of my grandfather, the one who lived most of his life in his tiny hometown, and even though his later years were spent outside the church, and even though he withdrew from much of town life towards the end, he would still mention to me how, like, the guy who fixed his car said he didn't have to pay right away, he could pay later, and my grandfather would say, "I just thought that was really special," in a manner that clearly went beyond money. And I believe he was getting a small need met, in the way his sad, gay, heartbroken granddaughter was getting a small need met entering dark bars to familiar faces a thousand miles away.

I don't find those interactions to be entirely whole-cloth different from the oft-maligned ones on the internet. Like, okay: As I'm writing this today, in the fall of 2022, I just got an updated booster shot. And days before, I'd posted online, "How are the side effects . . . ?" and both friends and strangers told me their experiences and they assuaged my anxiety and I felt better. Just now, I posted again to add my own experience to the mix, and that feels nice too. (I'm doing fine thanks, just a tad woozy.)

---

* Maybe one of you is reading this? You know me by a different name, I know. It's a long story. I'll tell you the whole thing sometime, if you want.

In middle school, I used to post on video game message boards when I was a weird, bullied, geeky kid, and that community was far better than the one I physically moved in at school. I used to be up at all hours as a teenager, and I'd hope someone on AIM or MSN Messenger was around to talk to—and often they were. I was such a lonely kid, both before and after I got the internet, and I hold no fondness for my youthful memories of being wide awake at midnight staring at the wall or calling the two friends with cellphones who stayed up late, hoping they'd answer. I hold no fondness for my insomniac childhood, going out of my mind with no outlet, none, zero, nothing, just darkness and blankness. Today, now, I do find it quietly moving, in a way I am only appreciating as I write this, that I can send out a little klaxon call on a platform and if some of my friends see it and feel like responding, they can, but they don't have to, either. Or even those not-quite-friends I have some loose connection to. (There's me not using that word *acquaintances* again, because I think *community* is better.)

Bink bink bink bink bink

A GUY JUST a few years older than me, a fellow Mennonite from the Pembina Valley, told me he'd once worked for CKMW, the country music station that serves the region. He worked evenings back then, and at about eleven or eleven thirty every night he'd get phone calls from farmers making song requests. "We didn't take song requests," he told me, "and they knew that, but they needed an excuse to talk. I heard from the same three guys regularly, but others would call as well. They mostly felt lonely. Sometimes they'd cry."

I think there are forever-ongoing symbioses between technology and loneliness, technology and community. "One could watch Jack Benny at 8 p.m. every Saturday night and know you're sharing the same moment with nearly every other American," Opus says. And yeah, that's true. And there's a certain melancholy ache to that. But there's limits to that melancholy's truth. How many people bond these days over prestige TV? Video games? I always think fondly of when Pokémon Go came out. I'm not a gamer, but walking around that summer, it felt like my neighbourhood had suddenly doubled in size.

Yes, we've lost things, good communal things, of course we have. For me, I'll offer the ritual of renting videos in a group as something beautiful I loved doing, something I weirdly miss in an aching way and which is never coming back. But I find it difficult to believe we don't always keep finding our own small versions of what Opus believed was lost, re-mutating and gelling into their own kind of salves.

Transsexuals

SOMETIMES THAT SALVE is circumstantial and disorganized, like chaotic chance meetings in bars or bonding online about vaccine side effects. Products of a sweet and quiet serendipity. Sometimes it's small, sometimes it doesn't actually take that much work.

...and then sometimes it takes a lot of work.

Two years ago, my friend Cat Fitzpatrick and I founded a publishing house, LittlePuss Press. Cat's a trans woman like myself. We publish many trans writers. When we threw our first event, it was indeed a book launch, but it also functioned as a gathering of trans people. It was in NYC in that summer of 2021, the newly post-vaccine days, where most of us had been deeply isolated for over a year, on top of the habitual isolation that outsizedly afflicts our communities.[4950]

At that book launch, trans people were the majority—an uncommon experience for any of us, being members of a dispersed population totalling around 0.5 percent of society. "I've never been in a room with this many trans people before," a girl said to me that night. And I'd heard this before at other trans readings too.

The euphoria and meaningfulness for us to be in that

space together … it was so palpable. It was palpable to me. I grew up not knowing a single person like myself. I came out at nineteen, and I did not find other trans people, plural, until I was twenty-four, when I had been trying to find others and failing for half a decade. (For Cat, she transitioned around 2000–2001, and her story holds a much longer version of that isolation.) I am grateful I am in community with other trans people now, and I also know what its absence feels like. I don't want to feel it again, and I don't want others to, either—we have enough else to worry about.

Cat and I began a press because we wanted to bring certain books into the world. But we also knew, from the get-go, that when you push art into the world, when you throw events, there is always a symbiosis with community of some kind. Even if you choose not to feed or seek it—which is a fair choice, pushing art into the world takes *so* much damn work on its own terms!—that symbiosis is still there, and we knew specifically what it looked like for trans books.

"I've never been in a room with this many trans people before." It pains me, to be honest, to still hear that sentence. I find the fact that it's such an exceptional experience to be a sad phenomenon. And so it is that as we run our weird little press, I will also do my best to give it devotion and care.

I FOUND THE Trans Ladies Picnic (TLP) inspiring in this respect. The TLP is a recurring event schemed up in 2011 by Red Durkin. The first one was in New York City and it has since spread far beyond. The idea was that even in a place like New York, it wasn't easy for trans women to just hang out and make friends, and a pot luck–style picnic could be a low-barrier way to do that. The idea was also flexibly simple: the only requirement to attend was to identify with the term *trans woman*. It's always been decentralized and DIY, so what they've looked like has varied by time and area, but every TLP I'm aware of has been collectively run, free to attend, in a public park, without any policing of who's allowed in, and bringing something was not a requirement. They're fun. And they too take work. Not tons, especially when a bunch of people chip in to do the organizing. But still. Certain women had to make them happen. And those women did. So it happened.

I was twenty-four when I went to my first one. I woke up not planning to go; I had to work an afternoon shift. And besides, I was nervous and anxious about what would happen if I went, *what-if-no-one-likes-me-what-if-no-one-talks-to-me-what-if-everyone-thinks-I'm-stupid*...you know. That kind of thing. I was so anxious about going. I almost didn't go. I got ready for work like normal and told the organizer I couldn't come. I thought about calling out sick. I called the automated system at work to do it, but, "I chickened out and ended the call before I could say I was calling out." That's what I wrote in my private journal that morning about how I wasn't going to go.

Then I called out for real last minute. I bought some shitty chips nobody would eat. I rode the subway for an hour down to Park Slope. I walked over a hill in Prospect Park with a plastic bag swinging around my arm. I was looking for two dozen people sitting in the grass. Prospect Park is big, and it was a bright summer Saturday. The park was packed. I thought it would be obvious, two dozen

transsexuals sitting in the grass. But it was not obvious.
From far away, it turned out we looked like any other
group of people. I had to look for longer than I thought.
Eventually I was sitting on blankets, and walking with
someone else to the bathroom and writing a postcard to a
woman in prison and listening, mostly listening, I didn't
speak that much at first, though I knew about four or five
girls there, all of whom had only recently appeared in my
life, all of whom melted in and out of the women I didn't
know, some of whom had just come out and some of
whom had been out for years, cooking every kind of
burger on a makeshift grill and throwing Frisbees, all with
bodies like mine, a kind of body I thought was shameful
and wretched and isolated, a burden I had to carry through
the world alone, this was at a picnic, it was simple, it
wasn't anything that complicated, you know what a picnic
is, don't you? I met this one woman and we talked for
hours, about art, politics, our educations, our families, and
as the sun lowered—when did that happen? I *literally* just
got here—a bunch of us including her walked to the house
of some girls who lived nearby with music and booze, then
she and I kissed in the bleary light of that Kensington
second-floor kitchen, which annoyed one of the girls in
the house because she and I had been hooking up, and
then the new girl and I got on a train and then she lay next
to me in my bed, gathering my hair in her hands.

Earlier in the day, back in the park, we took a picture
of all of us. The girl who took it had been quiet that afternoon, in men's clothes and bright-red nail polish. I
assumed she took the picture because she herself didn't
want to be photographed. But truly, who knows. She
showed up at the following year's picnic too, and she *was*

in that picture, wearing a long black shirt-dress and thick eye makeup. And then I never saw her again. There is still so much about all those women I don't know.

Recently, I found the picture from that first TLP of mine. There are exactly twenty of us in there. I remember most of their names, but not all. Two of those twenty are dead, from suicide, the future news of which arrived in early morning and nighttime phone calls that ripped apart the world (rest in peace). Three of those twenty, we still regularly talk, and I call them dear friends, including the girl who came to my bed. A decade later, it's all still too much to think about. These things changed my life.

SURVIVAL.

I was once in a private Facebook group that banded together to bail a trans woman in Iowa out of jail. Mira Bellwether (who has also since passed on, rest in peace) was the one who physically went to get her. "I made sure she ate well that night," she wrote later, "and with another trans woman, in a strange city. Our collective ability to make things happen is real. It changes lives."[51]

She added: "We put trans sisters in physical houses with their names on the door. We fund god knows how many surgeries not just for each other but for our siblings and cousins and even our ungrateful blood families. There is strength in working together and in asking for help." Yes.

And then also: "Here's what any of us can do differently: we can swallow our pride a little bit more and tell everyone how bad things are when they are bad. This doesn't ruin community, it's what creates community." Yes. This was in the context of her suffering from the cancer that took her, and how others weren't reaching out.

So Look, What the Hell Is Water?

I HAVE BEEN embroiled in many trans communities through the last decade. Here's a story of another one.

In 2014, a trans-run publishing house called Topside Press put out my first book.[52] They sent me and others on long book tours around the US, Canada, the UK, and Ireland. They were more like seat-of-the-pants *band* tours, honestly—we crashed on couches, shared spare beds, sold zines for gas money, that kind of thing.

We did many readings to majority-trans audiences. I heard variations on that sentence, "I've never been around this many trans people before." I saw that same wonder on many faces. We read to an art gallery of a hundred people in Calgary and a living room of two dozen in Dallas; we read to a pub in Edinburgh and a uni hall in Sheffield and a graffitied warehouse in Dublin. The idea, inspired by the old Sister Spit tours,* was that anywhere someone wanted to host us, so long as you could put us up and deliver a crowd, we would come to your town and do a reading and

---

* A travelling road show of queer art begun by Michelle Tea, which still lives on today.

any local queer writers were invited to read with us. So that's what we did. We showed up and slept in the houses of so many people we had never met. So many of those same people I still today call friends. It all sounds overtly romantic thinking about it now, but it happened and it worked. In fall 2014 in particular, Sybil Lamb and I drove more than ten thousand miles around the US and Canada doing thirty-seven shows* and it was a gauntlet and it was wild and I loved it. But I don't know if I thought too deeply about the community aspect of it. It was happening, it was great, I was on a book tour, it was my first book, writers are supposed to do book tours, aren't they? The community implications of what was happening, the power of it, only settled on me after the fact, like the proverbial young fish in David Foster Wallace's lecture, passing an older fish who says, "Morning boys, how's the water?" causing one young fish to say to the other, "What the hell is water?"[53]

That small-town principal uncle of mine? The one who said, "I've lived there twenty years and I still don't feel like I'm from there"? He told me a funny story once: So one day, he's driving his van to school, which is a five-minute trip. But halfway there, he runs out of gas— he'd thought my aunt had filled up the tank, but the gas gauge was broken. So as he's trundling to the side of the road, a guy pulls up beside him. My uncle knows him; in fact, the guy's kid goes to his school. "Hi, Garth. Need a push?" "That . . . would be great." In the time it takes him to get out and start pushing, two *other* guys, both of whom are *also* dads at my uncle's school, have stopped and recognized him, and they get out and push too.

* After which Sybil and I permanently tied our lives together, but that's a whole other story!

So there's three grown men pushing a van down the street, ferrying the town principal to work.

My uncle was mortified but also told this story with great amusement. I wonder if he felt like he was from there that day. I wonder if that question of belonging and community occurred to him. Or if it was, "Water, what the hell is water?" Maybe I should ask him what he thinks about that. Maybe I will before I finish writing this.

I do remember him telling me that story with warmth, which makes plenty of sense; there are so many opportunities in this big world to run out of gas where no one's going to help you.

Topside Press only existed for a short time, publishing books between 2012 and 2017, and it thrived on the community that surrounded it. Its first book was an anthology of twenty-seven trans fiction writers, edited by two trans men, Riley MacLeod and The Guy. Those two, plus Red Durkin and Julie Blair, both trans women, were the public face of it in the beginning years, and others helped a bunch behind the scenes—Katie Liederman, Zo Holmes, Sarah Schulman. Probably others I'm forgetting. Cat, my current LittlePuss partner, she ran it in the end years, and I co-edited the other press anthology with her. Factoring in everyone who hosted tour events, or put up authors, or packed book mail or did graphic design or folded chapbooks or copyedited whole books, possibly over a hundred people at some point donated labour to the Topside project, and plenty more were physically there to witness and participate in it.

Imogen Binnie wrote a novel for Topside called *Nevada* that became an instant cult classic ("The book that cracked a thousand eggs"[54] in the modern parlance) and

vaulted her into a world of TV and film. She wrote later
that those years "were intoxicating ... I remember many,
many Bud Light Lime-A-Ritas* in what felt like an end-
less, endlessly hot and humid Brooklyn summer, talking
shit all night about representation, literature, trans literature, how to be trans in the world, bodies, intersectionality,
and what could be salvaged from transphobic seventies
and eighties feminism."[55] I was there too, for a lot of it,
and it did all feel like we were doing stuff together. "It felt
like we were doing it within *our community*,"[56] Imogen
recounted to me years later (emphasis mine).

It really was an intensely special time. And as I said, *so*
many people donated their energy and their labour to it.
It was a lovely thing to witness.

The press had many problems in its orbit. The whole
story of Topside could fill a book on its own, but to glanc-
ingly summarize for The Record†: There was certainly
infighting, lots of pain over breakups, financial skuldug-
gery, and some inexcusably shitty interpersonal behaviour
(that trans arts gathering I mentioned, with the organizer
accused of abuse and the failed accountability process?
Also a Topside thing). What felt welcoming to some could
feel alienating and overly cool-kid to others, and it got out
over its skis claiming Authentic Trans Representation,
particularly given its whiteness.

Anything else ...? Ah yes, also, one day The Guy decided
to ghost and close up shop and suddenly the whole thing
was over.

....

* Bud Light Lime-A-Ritas and Straw-Ber-Ritas became staple boozy beverages
of the TLP in the mid-2010s. Why did this happen?? I still have no idea.

† For all other accounts of shittiness, well, if you really want to know, come
accost me in the flesh.

See, another thing about the press is that The Guy owned the actual legal entity, which was a standard private business set up the way those things are. He had sole control over everything, which no one really talked about. And he wouldn't give that control up, even as he called it quits, and that meant the entire project went away despite the wishes of many. That's why it only existed those few years. Why The Guy was done, I don't know, and I probably never will. While the press was running, few of us acknowledged aloud that The Guy actually had the keys to the car, that when push came to shove, it was all his, and indeed that fact often led to friction when his exuberance and charisma turned into domineering abrasiveness, which also happened often.

The paradox is that the infrastructure of this press was at once community-oriented and controlled by one man, without whose approval little happened. The energy and labour this project gathered—of which I include my own—was beautifully communal and exploitative at the same time. That paradox never really occurred to me either when the press was functional, even during my own spats with The Guy. (Water? What the hell is water?)

Assumptions (4)

AROUND THE TAIL end of this time, I got that book publicist job with Biblioasis. In this position, I was charged with advocating for the work of our authors. In other words, promotion and sales.

As I'd sit around with my co-workers, divining just how the hell to publicize an upcoming book, we'd often come back to community. Remembering my Topside experience, I'd often bring it back to community. "We need to engage the [X] community!" I'd say. (There I was, deploying and nodding to this phrase I now dislike.)

The whole thing could get esoteric—"the deep-sea diving community" is a phrase that has unironically left my mouth—but sometimes it alluded to larger, more cohesive forces, like "the Catholic community." Regardless, it was my past experience in a trans literary scene—itself just one spoke in the wheel of larger trans communities— that led me to believe I knew how to do this, to stoke excitement for a book within a focused group of people to whom the book might appeal. I thought this would be a simpler aspect of this new job I had.

These efforts sometimes worked! Sometimes they failed. But regardless, I had immediate assumptions that:

- a cohesive and singular community existed around experiences spoken to by the book;
- I could then devise a method to alert that community about the book;
- members of that community would then buy the book.

Those assumptions were swift, and they were often wrong—even on the occasions that promotional success ensued. Now, Biblioasis is an indie house which then had a staff of six—not exactly a consultant-stocked behemoth—and there's limits to how much I can extrapolate from my individual experience there. But I still think about our assumptive invocations of "the [X] community," and that term as I see it used from Netflix to the *New York Times*. And. Well. I wonder. About the prevalence of these assumptions. About the deepness of that prevalence. The idea that, for a given subject or experience, a singular community exists, and there's ways to talk to that community, and their community could be your audience, your customers. As I grow older, I see the enormousness of these assumptions, and wonder how silently threaded they are through the world. Noor Naga again: *"Those outside of a language, a culture, see furniture through a window and believe it is a room. But those inside know there are infinite rooms just out of view, and that they can always be more deeply inside."*

Exceptional

IT MIGHT FURTHER be tempting, with the whole Topside business, to look back and say, "You know, that wasn't really community in the end. It was one guy's stuff." There'd be some truth to that. But it wouldn't make the real community that happened during those years vanish, either.

What I've understood since Topside went down the tubes: how unexceptional its story is. As I was completing a draft of this essay, the indie literary organization Catapult suddenly announced it would close its online magazine and writing classes and focus on its book publishing program.[57] It did this without first informing its active teachers, students, and staff.[58] One teacher I know was getting a massage when the news broke—this went down on Valentine's Day, no less—and was paying at the end when she received a concerned text from a neighbour who'd heard the news. That's how she discovered she no longer had a job.

I'd always loved Catapult's work. They delivered interesting, tough literature in the magazine. Sofia Samatar's meditation on social media, for instance, is one of my all-time favourite essays (read it![59]). Or there's Marina Benjamin's *Insomnia,* a beautiful book-length essay on its

titular thorny subject. As a professional, I'd also been
wowed by the high figures they paid their teachers, which
is a *very rare thing to utter* about an institution of creative
writing pedagogy.

What I didn't know: Catapult was founded by Elizabeth Koch, daughter of Charles Koch, the billionaire CEO
of Koch Industries and political mega-donor to right-wing
causes. Shortly after Catapult's recent announcement,
the *New York Times* ran a profile on Koch that revealed
her to be deep in the self-help/wellness world. If I can get
a little personal here, I found the ideas she preached to be
pseudo-scientific grift, stuff I consider quite opposite to
the wisdom in literary work like Samatar's and Benjamin's. For instance, Koch's new big idea is "the Perception
Box," a term she has trademarked:

> We all live inside an invisible but ever-present men-
> tal box—a Perception Box ... This box distorts our
> perceptions of everything and everyone around us.
> It distorts our ability to understand other people, to
> see them clearly, to connect with them. And it dis-
> torts our ability to really even know ourselves.[60]

Soon after all this went down, Catapult's book publishing website proclaimed they will only put out work "that
engages with our Perception Box, the powerful metaphor
we use to define the structure and boundaries of how we
see others in their full humanity, and invites new ways of
seeing and being seen."[61]

Right.

Thinking back to the magazines and classes: Catapult
held a community of teachers, students, a staff—not

unlike Topside, that community existed, it did stuff for years, and it was real. And then came a decision from the person who owned things. The teacher from above told me in an email: "It really reinforced that even when a community feels sturdy and somewhat self-sustaining (the school made money!) the whims of the person at the top can dismantle it in a moment."

I wonder how Koch thought she might weld her Perception Box concept onto that community—at least, those she hadn't fired via press release. The *Times* profile, which I'd challenge anyone to characterize as anything but a puff piece, certainly didn't ask. The communities she helmed then vaporized were not present. The Catapult closures were mentioned only once, in a parenthetical.

Thriving and nurturing communities are often beholden to powerful entities over which, truly, there was always little control. For instance: There are a few bars in New York City right now that host regular trans fundraisers and artistic open mics. These events are wonderful spaces. They fund surgeries and housing and nourish art and life. I love the reliability these spaces have made! I love what they do for trans communities! These events are also dependent on these particular bars.

Now. Certainly, I'd rather depend on them than the whims of Elizabeth Koch or The Guy. But bars are also dependent on New York real estate. Bars tend to close. Gay bars, especially, tend to close.[62] It's not unexceptional.

Ghost World

THERE'S A FAST-FOOD coffee chain in Canada that's expanded rapidly in recent decades. They surpassed McDonald's by sales in 2002, and they currently operate twice the locations per capita as the Golden Arches do in the United States. For my Canadian readers, plus anybody who's spent so much as an airport's hour in the country, you know what I'm talking about: Tim Hortons. It is materially and comically impossible to avoid Tim's in our contemporary national life. Driving to our house in Windsor, the five-mile trip from the Detroit tunnel takes you directly past *four* of them, not including a fifth that's a short walk past our home.

Tim's functions as a de facto third place* in much of the country. Which makes sense: they're inexpensive, open late, Canada has a housing crisis that is *not* improving, plus, you know, it's cold around here! So, not too surprising it's become a common location of gathering. Tim's is where old guys meet their retired pals and teenagers gab after school and I complete a Facebook Marketplace deal and crowded families leave the house on the cheap.

....

* *Third place* refers to a social space outside the twin environments of home or work, such as cafés, gyms, libraries, bars, churches, community centres, and the like.

I don't mean to romanticize any of this—my individual Canadian life has led me to find Tim's *very depressing,* and some of these needs, like those brought on by the housing crisis, are a symptom of societal failure that no third place can fix. Yet the facts are, Tim's does what it does, and it fascinates me how a boring coffee chain has provided this function for so many. And, of course, Tim Hortons is also a multinational conglomerate that exists to make money. So. I wonder about this function's fragility too, in this way. One of the eerier feelings from the early pandemic was when Tim's went drive-thru-only and I couldn't walk into one.

Today, long after society has "reopened," a number of fast-food joints have kept their dining rooms closed and / or opened new takeout-and-delivery-only locations. From *Slate:*

Name a fast-food restaurant and the odds are the company has recently developed a branch without any restaurant at all. Chipotle's first "Digital Kitchen," which opened in upstate New York in 2020, has no dining room. A branch that opened last year in the Cleveland suburbs doesn't even let customers inside the store. This summer, Taco Bell opened something it calls Taco Bell Defy, which is not a restaurant at all but a purple taco tollbooth powered by QR code readers and dumbwaiters that bring the food down from a second-story kitchen. The operation is, by most accounts, astoundingly efficient . . . the shared spaces that emptied out during the pandemic are slow to fill back up, to the point that walk-up, dine-in customers like me are no longer the focus, and might even be a nuisance. *Often*

*lauded as a vital "third space" for seniors, teenagers, and
families in communities that lack friendly public spaces,*
McDonald's unveiled a concept store in 2020 that
has no seating at all.[63] (emphasis mine)

I found this article riding the subway home on an early
Sunday evening in New York. I had just gone to a church
service at Manhattan Mennonite Fellowship, one of the
first in-person services I'd attended since the pandemic
began. There was a Starbucks around the corner I liked to
sit and work in, so I ordered a drink in advance on their app
and I headed there, feeling buoyed by a good service and
the community it provided. It felt deeply good to be around
people again, and the last thing I wanted was to sit in my
room alone. Then I walked into the Starbucks and found
all the chairs were gone. The counters butted up against
empty space. I asked the girl working what happened.
"We're no longer dine-in," she said. "Sorry." She was nice.
I think she sensed that the emptiness had me unsettled.
She said, apologetically, "I think there's one on First Avenue that's still dine-in?" I walked out with my drink that I
bought digitally and facelessly (joke's on me) and checked
the one on First Avenue—it was closing soon. I walked
over to another coffee shop in the neighbourhood I knew
to be open late on Sundays, but it was empty inside. A
scribbled sign on their window told me they'd changed
their hours to close earlier. A lone employee inside was
sweeping up among the chairs on tables.

I still had my stupid Starbucks drink. It was getting
dark. *Why do you need to work in a fucking café so badly
anyway?* I thought to myself. *At home you have a bedroom
with a desk. Go work at it. That's what it's there for! What's*

the big deal? I got on the subway and found that *Slate* article. I read it and went home to my apartment to sit in my
room alone.

MONTHS LATER, THE *Wall Street Journal* reported further
on this phenomenon, fast-food restaurants with no
restaurant. There was an official McDonald's statement
in this one: "We value the space and community our traditional restaurants create, so restaurants with dine-in
service are and will continue to be an important way we
serve our communities."

Nice move there, invoking community twice in a sentence, no? About as farcical, I'd hazard, as Adobe pleading,
"Casey, you're still part of the Adobe community!" See,
that *Journal* article had detailed an experimental new
drive-thru-only McDonald's in Texas featuring a fully
automated delivery system: "When you pull up to the
window in the 'order ahead' lane, a conveyor delivers
your food or beverage with help from a robotic arm that
pushes the bag out to the waiting car."[64]

No wonder the McDonald's statement desperately piv-
oted to emphasize community, insisting that dine-in
service wasn't dead yet. I would pivot in such Orwellian
fashion too, if that's the ghost world of a future I was
charged with defending: No human attached to your
food, no flesh, no face, no room to sit in encumbered by
bothersome people with their bothersome livelihoods.
Just you sitting in your car, you with your own bothersome livelihood, you, alone, reaching for a paper bag
from a robotic arm, alone.

What's Water

...BUT PERHAPS I'M veering a bit into Opus-like melancholy myself.

Let me finish planting my stake in the ground.

I think there's a powerful undertow in society that says, *What if community makes you pathetic and weak?* I think there are subwoofer-volume forces saying, *Live by your own grit and resources!* (And sometimes not so subwoofer-volume.) I think the very real quiet strength that everyday humans can make out of hard situations through their own grit and resources—individualism, let's say—gets cruelly leveraged into quiet voices asking, *Why can't you take care of yourself on your own? Are you just pathetic, weak?*

Now: Individualism can be powerful, yeah. I don't want to diminish the individual resilience and dignity that we as humans carry within us. It's real. But I would also posit that the extreme examples of long-term individualism, those which delve into asceticism and hermitude—I think of the "Last Hermit" in Maine who lived in the forest for fifteen years without speaking to another human[65]—such outlier exceptions prove the rule: the overwhelming majority of us cannot live without the support of others. What's the symbiosis between communitarianism and individualism? I think the loving paradox goes something like this: Sure, you can take care of yourself, but you can't do it on your own.

FOR ME, PERSONALLY, I had queer experiences, tangled as they were, that birthed the direction of my life, and my ears prick to the same. Cecilia Gentili* said once of her queer activism: "In treatment, one of the counselors told me that I have to find something I enjoy as much as that feeling of shooting heroin. And that came to be community and working for my community."[66] Chelsey Johnson wrote once of being a lesbian in 1990s Portland: "...when I walked into any of these places someone knew me. Someone *knew* me. We knew each other. I've never known anything like it and won't again. To recognize someone anywhere you go. To recognize each other everywhere: the coffee shop, the sidewalk, the bicycle commute, the bookstore, the bar."[67]

That salve and strength is real. It can take so many different surprising shapes, but it's real, as real as the problem it soothes. ("A risk that rivals smoking.") There's no part of me that can forget those book tours in the mid-2010s. They weren't just youthful larks, as fun as they were, they built community, and people worked to make them happen and they didn't have to. If you are one of those people who took us into your home, or put together a venue, or fed us meals or read with us or drank with us till late or did a workshop or made us coffee in the morn-

....

* A legendary NYC trans/immigrant/sex work activist and author (whom we published at LittlePuss, her book *Faltas* rules). She's particularly done a lot to fund trans health services in New York State. At a book launch, I once saw a girl ask Cecilia to sign her new boobs in thanks. She did!

ings and sent us on our way, I will always be grateful to you and I will never forget you. Several of you have since died (rest in peace), all of you far too young, all of you transsexual women, and I will never forget you either.

And if you just simply came, if you just showed up with your body and sat in the corner and left without saying a word—I know that maybe it wasn't an accident. I know you didn't have to come. Maybe you even called in sick to work last-minute that night. What the hell is water? You get to a certain point and you know what's water. Cat, my LittlePuss partner, she organized that tour, and she later said of that time period: "I dragged myself out of a deep depression about the meaninglessness of my life that I had previously been experiencing."[68] Some years later, I posted a fond memory about the tours, and one of the kids from that living room in Dallas left a comment: "That night changed my life."

Interlude

SO THOSE ARE some personal truths for how I think about community:

It consists of both enumeration and mythos.

It's always dissolving and remaking itself.

It contains multiplicities and inner divides, sometimes more than an outsider could ever conceive of.

It is always capable of toxicity while also being necessary for the existence of a life worth living.

Much is revealed when a community asks what it does not want to look at.

A Minimum Viable Community

I RECENTLY LEARNED about the concept of hacker houses, the Silicon Valley–inflected take on communal house living.* I did not learn about them in a warm context. I read about Launch House, a hacker house started by Americans renting coastal digs in Mexico and letting out rooms to wannabe start-up founders, who "had to do the following: Pay rent, launch projects and build their company in public."[69]

Eventually they did this in a mansion in Beverly Hills. You had to pay three thousand dollars to join a month-long cohort. When members got in, they did "a team-building exercise called the 'Founders' Circle' that mimics religious confessionals. Each member is encouraged to share the most difficult experiences of their lives—deaths of loved ones, sexual assaults, grave financial losses—a practice that employees refer to as 'trauma bonding'." Members

....

* Hacker houses are big houses stuffed with tech entrepeneurs and engineers and start-up employees, usually young people with big dreams hustling non-stop who want community to hustle with. I'm kind of fascinated with the idea—I always associate communal houses with the hippies and co-ops of my Pacific Northwest youth, the kinds with, like, chore wheels and bulk vegan staples.

had to publicly boost the community and were rewarded for doing so. Women were usually a minority in these cohorts. They reported being sexually assaulted in the house. They reported boozy parties with hundreds of possibly underaged girls wandering in and passing out outside. One member talked of a party where she and other women were seemingly roofied.[70] A different member overdosed one morning and had to go to the hospital, and after the ambulance pulled away, one of the founders got on the phone. Figuring out care for the member on his way to the hospital? Contacting loved ones? Nope, landing fintech TikTok investors for the New York cohort.

An *ABC Money* article on Launch House is headlined, "How Launch House is Redefining the Global *Community*."[71] A *Zenger* article in *Forbes* gushes: "Members are signing up for not just a predictable rate of return, but a *community* that mentors and builds experience with one another."[72] Launch House's landing page, as of the publication of this essay, contains exactly one sentence: "A *community-driven*, early-stage venture fund for the New Silicon Valley."[73] (All emphases mine.)

As Rebecca Jennings, who wrote a *Vox* exposé detailing the above grossness, put it:

> Community, insists the Web3 startup that sells digital coins ... "community," says the mobile banking app targeting digital creators and other freelancers whose main uniting factor is that they work alone; "community" say the members of Launch House when what they are referring to are customers.

* * *

I'VE BEGUN TO see community in the context of sales and promotion everywhere, and it's a bit different from what I detailed at Biblioasis. There, we were trying to find communities to reach, but in this iteration, companies are trying to convince people they're part of a new community altogether. It's not just me—both word and concept are verifiably receiving their Madison Avenue moments in the sun.[74] Convincing people they're a part of something is a great way to get their money! Sometimes the shape this takes is laughably inane ("Casey, you're still a part of the Adobe community!") and sometimes, like with Launch House, it's ... quite gravely not.

But either way, the idea's literally serious business. There's a thing now in start-up land called "minimum viable community." It applies the idea of a minimum viable product* to a community that uses or works on the product. There's a *Forbes* editorial breaking it down. "Pick your biggest problem," it suggests as a first step, "and build a community around this." It makes so much sense, doesn't it? Community makes us feel good, everybody knows that. Community is healthy, right? Community can solve big problems, right? Everybody knows that. Shouldn't we be thinking of efficient, effective ways to build and calibrate communities? Shouldn't we harness all our human knowledge to build better communities? Shouldn't we? Shouldn't we?

....

* A minimum viable product is proof-of-concept applied to software: find a simple bare-bones way to test-drive your product in the real world and learn from its successes and failures, then proceed to scale your idea accordingly.

Real Community

I MEAN, YES, we should. But in particular the implosion and toxicity of co-working start-ups selling "community," not just Launch House but also places like WeWork[75] and The Wing[76][77], give me pause. As much as it's easy for someone like me to scorn such moneyed corporate spaces—like, I am a trans, leftist book person who rarely throws events for more than a few dozen people at a time—I do still brood about the cautionary tales of such implosions. "Pick your biggest problem, and build a community around this." That phrasing makes my skin *itch*. I can tell you why.

"People from lonely backgrounds are most prone to joining a cult," said a former member of Launch House, one of whose founders was fascinated by organized religion, and once extolled how the organization could learn from how it proselytized (think of the "trauma bonding" required of new members). Jennings ends her piece with this:

As more companies raise money for projects promising so-called community, Launch House may very well be a frightening bellwether. True community-building, as tech founders should have realized by now, requires more than renting a mansion in Beverly Hills ... It's more than tweeting hustle porn and hosting parties. Sometimes, community is what happens when a great deal of eager young people come together and realize the people who brought them there have no idea how to build a community at all.

Now, my sympathies lie largely with Launch House's critics and Jennings's overall points. But there was something to her exposé I don't think is quite correct: the idea of "true community-building." The implication, in her story, being that Launch House only aspired or pretended to build community, but the callousness that undergirded those aspirations and the violence it tolerated rendered it something else, in the end.

I've often sensed a No True Scotsman* fallacy creep into our conversations around community. I've certainly echoed the idea myself: that if a community is rooted in dishonourable intentions or false pretenses, if a community allows cruelty to its vulnerable members or unduly casts them out—well then, it's not *really* community, is it?

Wrong. It is. This is also what communities do. Always have, always will. Communities welcome certain people and cast a suspicious eye on others. Communities lift up their valued members and ignore those they value a bit

....

* The No True Scotsman fallacy refers to a rhetorical sleight of hand in which a person alters the definition of what constitutes a *true* [insert subject here] to keep that definition morally pure, often to the point of ignoring verifiable facts on the ground. Steven Pinker gives "No true Christian ever kills" as an example. I'll throw in my own: "No true feminist is transphobic." (E.g., that world sounds nice, but it's not the one we live in.)

less. Sometimes those values are, shall we say, suspect. Communities can expel members when they choose, regardless of what that means for the member, and they stay communities no matter how heartless that expulsion might be. A high school football team is a community and so is a high school musical cast and so is a group of activist-artists and so are those same artists when they defend an abusive member. A gated neighbourhood pushing out undesirables is a community and so is a small town that keeps horrid secrets and so is the collection of Christian nationalists moving to North Idaho with visions of the American Redoubt that celebrates leaders who celebrate the Confederacy alongside former legislators who protest Pride parades and want a "Holy Army" in the USA.[78] Why are these Christian nationalists moving out to North Idaho? Because, says a local professor, "they want to be around people that are like them."[79] Ah, community. It can arise out of every intent, from grift to racism to the cold calculations of a start-up founder to the dreams of the power-mad. No healing qualities of goodness required. *We'll handle it in the church.*

I'm trying to say that to be in community with others is in many ways a *quotidian action*, equally capable of cruelty and health in the way of many ordinary things, mundane actions that happen every day with the capacity for both salve and sickness. Humans need community, but there's no good assuming it's always a conduit for goodness.

This isn't just semantics either. In order to prevent, say, events like the sexual assaults at Launch House or zealots protesting our Prides, we have to understand what communities are capable of. A community is sometimes just a vehicle for the most powerful forces within it. Doing community work under the assumption that community is ipso facto Good—it can inure one to the potential pitfalls of the work.

Part of me wants to reach for metaphors here. Maybe, say, community is like a tool, and any tool operator needs to understand the hazards that can accompany the tool's use. Or maybe, say, when we discover a community has been callous and we say, "That's not really community," perhaps that's like declaring a car that hit a pedestrian is no longer a car.

But another part of me knows the truth is tougher, darker, and even more complicated. Because the definitions of what's callous or cruel can vary greatly from one community to the next. And those definitions, and how much we care about them, can shift and wobble and fold in on themselves from within a community too. If you've ever been in a group where someone does something shitty and everyone shrugs their shoulders—*What can you do? What did you expect?*—you know what I mean. There are narratives we are drawn to, that we choose, and there are narratives we don't want to look at.

The Mennonite Thing

WHEN I WAS in college, I took a lit course that featured *A Complicated Kindness* by Manitoban author Miriam Toews, a novel about the Steinbach region, that cluster of Mennonite burgs from where my mother's family springs. *A Complicated Kindness* is a beautiful, hilarious, and painful book—about a teenaged girl named Nomi who, at the book's outset, is in grief over her mother's and sister's sudden and mysterious departures. Nomi's father deals by withdrawing into himself, and Nomi deals by manically crashing around town, fighting with her idiot boyfriend, getting angrily drunk and high, and slowly drawing the ire of the church that governs its fundamentalist people. It all builds to a heart-shocking, hopeful, and devastating ending that I won't spoil, but which also holds lessons about community.

It's expertly written, and it's my favourite book. I didn't grow up in its world, but my mother did, and I spent my childhood at that world's edge. It was strange to discuss the book in a brutalist university building in downtown Portland, Oregon.

In that class, I spoke of my personal relation to the material. And a bright-eyed girl approached me afterwards in the hall. She said she wanted to know more about Mennonites. She said that the Mennonite way of life "really sounds like how I want to live."

This girl was a young, hippie-inflected, artsy type, someone I might have pictured in a communal house with chore wheels and bulk vegan staples. She was enraptured by the idea of rural off-the-grid living, and she wanted to know what I could tell her about that.

And I could tell her nothing. Nothing! I mean, first of all, the Mennonites in Toews's novel didn't even live communally or off-the-grid, they had individual houses and cars and telephones, which didn't seem to register to my classmate. But more disturbingly, neither did the fact that the book was concerned with the misery such communities could inflict on young, bright-eyed people like her. Like—she had idealizations at the ready, and a voice from the source warning against them was not going to get in the way.

I'm stuck on this phenomenon. I'm stuck on how non-Mennonites can be fascinated with us in a way that disquiets me. It happens all the time. It's the reason there are Amish reality shows and the bonnet-ripper book genre* and the American cover of Toews's novel *Women Talking* features a big, stark, faceless series of women in traditional black dress and head coverings. I'm too aware, from my life as a transsexual, of what it's like when some-

* Immense hat-tip to the podcast *Just Plain Wrong* featuring three Mennonite librarians painstakingly breaking down nearly every representation of Mennonites and Amish people in popular culture, and widening my eyes to the cultural reach of this phenomenon. If any of you three are reading this, I love your podcast, you are doing the Lord's work.

one finds you Interesting—or rather, when you *represent* Interesting, rather than you, yourself, a strange individual human. Now: Mennonites are not a minority under attack in Canada and the US, the way many minorities are. But. It disquiets me, this fascination. Jonathan Dyck, a fellow Mennonite author in Winnipeg, once related to me:

> I've lived in a few other cities and been lucky enough to find myself around dinner tables or at parties with left-leaning folks who tend to fetishize community (like they love talking about setting up communes and living outside the flows of Capital, etc., etc., but also would maybe be kind of disastrous in those types of spaces . . .) and they are delighted/intrigued to learn I'm Mennonite . . . I can't help myself (and I'm usually a bit drunk in these situations) so I end up talking waaaaay too much, and what was at first a fun little novelty turns into a long, potentially heavy convo that no one asked for.

Or, as Margaret Steffler wrote about her experiences teaching Mennonite literature: "I am all too aware that readers not only want 'the Mennonite thing,' but crave it as if it will somehow satisfy vague expectations and even longings."[80]

Even longings.

Don't we all have those.

There's something about *assumptions* I keep coming back to, the assumption of innocence and goodness, of falling in love with the idea of community, of how you think others *must* be living, and what that can lead you to ignore.

* * *

MIRIAM TOEWS'S FATHER and sister both died by suicide. She has written extensively, outside fictional realms, about her family among that Mennonite community that both she and my family come from. Excerpts from her essay "Peace Shall Destroy Many"*:

My father had a nervous breakdown at the age of seventeen and was diagnosed with bipolar disorder, then called manic depression. His family never spoke of it except to berate him for being weak and effeminate and not devout enough a Christian, even though he attended church relentlessly, taught Sunday school, prayed his heart out for relief and never missed a sermon

(...)

My grandmother, my father's mother, was a secret alcoholic. Our community was dry, drinking was a sin, but she shoplifted bottles of vanilla extract from the local grocer and drank them one by one alone in the darkness of her small apartment. My parents would let themselves in with a key that they kept, pick her up, clean her up and put her to bed. My mother had mentioned to me that she suspected that my grandmother had been assaulted by a group of local men when she was a young woman, but it was never spoken of, never investigated. Every few weeks, the owner of the grocery store where my grandmother stole vanilla would call my father and tell him the sum total of

* The title of her essay refers to the seminal 1962 Mennonite novel of the same name by Rudy Wiebe. Much of Toews's essay is about Wiebe, a man who also, in his work, incisively examined community.

the missing bottles—he never confronted my
grandmother directly—and my father would write
him a cheque and that was that, until the next time,
when the same process would be repeated.

Yet again. A community functioning how it was
intended—keeping peace, preventing rifts, making problems go away. My uncle, the small-town principal, told
me once that the shoplifting-vanilla thing still happens in
town. A grocer he knew said it still happened.

My mother and stepfather both left their respective
Mennonite churches as adults, and my father was excom-
municated from his. None of them talked about any of it,
not when I was growing up, anyway. But over the years, I
sensed a suspicion in each of them of what they perceived
as organized groups of people, especially people who
believed in something, believed in something dearly and
wholeheartedly. When I came out in college, my mother
believed I'd been taken in by a bad crowd. "You're going
to this new university, and who knows what they're telling you there!" Or when I joined the Portland Gay Men's
Chorus, we went on a trip to Boise, Idaho, and she said
with uncharacteristic sharpness, "You're doing a recruit-
ment trip! Well, that's what it is!", ironically echoing the
kind of homophobic language used by the religious con-
servatives she decried, and she tells me now, fifteen years
later, that she has no memory of saying this. (I believe
her.) When she said it all those years ago, it was in that
very same house in the cul-de-sac surrounded by neighbours to whom she couldn't get through. Centuries ago,
in the birth of Mennonitism during the Reformation,
when Mennonites were persecuted and burned at the

stake, they believed that church services could be held in the plainest of rooms and that anybody could be a minister. "For where two or three gather in my name, there am I with them."[81] (Jesus said that.)

My grandmother, my father's mother, always said her small-town upbringing represented her best years. She never stopped speaking fondly of her youth. And she once told me that her father, my great-grandfather, was very progressive, very kind, let her do much even though she was a girl, except for wearing pants or going to school. She really wanted to go to school. And she was extraordinarily smart. But she was born in the 1930s and she was in Winkler, Manitoba, and certain things just wouldn't be happening for her. And also she loved her upbringing, she wouldn't trade it for the world. Even *A Complicated Kindness* has a line about the mother character, Trudie, who the book strongly implies ended up killing herself:

> Trudie had her kids and her husband and her books. She had a car and nightgowns and white lace curtains. She had friends. She had equanimity. Everything was good. She lived in a town where every single person knew who she was and where she came from and sometimes that made her crazy but most of the time she liked that because it made her feel like she was a part of something.[82]

My grandmother also mentioned once, when she and I were alone, that there was a kid in her town who "was ... L—G—B—T?" She drew out the letters questioningly. Quietly she said, "We used to ..." She covered her mouth and in a pantomime snickered and pointed. "He killed himself." She began to look resigned, telling me this. "I hope things are better now."

There's a line from a Venita Blackburn story: *"We sometimes make compromises, invite poison into our lives, and it can't be helped."*[83] In one of my grandmother's last emails, when she could still do that, she reiterated of her childhood, "I only have good memories. Really, they were all good." Her memory was failing her by then, but still, I could only believe her.

Darkness

I'VE TALKED LARGELY of small communities in this essay, so far, communities with little power outside their own worlds. I haven't talked much about community in the way of society's majorities, the majorities with actual power.

Now and then, I go on a date with a man I am attracted to, or I am even just in bed for a hookup, or even I'm just randomly propositioned by a man I don't immediately dislike. And suddenly, the world feels different. Particularly when that man is not aware that I am trans—which is even rarer, but truly, suddenly the entire world is wholecloth different. Bartenders treat me differently. Strangers on the street, their body language is different. I walk to the bathroom in a restaurant and I can feel myself walking differently, and in the mirror I see a softer, happier, more restful woman. It's like a puzzle you never found the last piece to but suddenly it turns up and the picture is complete out of nowhere. Every song, every movie, and, beyond that, every piece of family lore and wisdom that rested on conventional heterosexuality—suddenly it all snaps into focus. All this culture and community that rested on men and women dating each other, all of it resting in the background for years, decades—now it all gets to apply to me. Like an aperture that was waiting so long for the right lens, like suddenly losing an accent and blending in as a native speaker.

Chelsea Johnson also wrote in *Stray City* about when her lesbian protagonist begins dating a man:

> *So this is what it's like*, I thought as we walked down the main street. *To hold hands and not garner a single glance. How strange.* It reminded me of one time at a show when, bored, Summer let me try on her six-inch platforms and suddenly the whole space was different. I inhabit a small body, five foot two. The world of shoulders is one I know well. But now I could see clearly, my head level with all the others, an unobstructed view ... *This is what it's like to be tall?* I had said in wonder and indignation and envy. *They just walk around able to see everything. And they take it for granted.*[84]

Later:

> It's the gays who say, We are everywhere, but straightness really was everywhere. The world was sodden with it. Versions of the relationship I was now in played out in everything ever written, acted, sung, sold, declared. The abundance of representation dizzied me. There was so much written and sold about the love and trouble between men and women that if you lined it all up end to end the whole world would be wrapped as thickly and totally as a rubberband ball.
>
> The unsolicited validation was stunning ... The billboards beamed down at me, *Yes, you.* The maga-

zine covers flaunted answers to questions I'd never thought to have.

And that is indeed how I feel. Like suddenly the culture of the world is intelligible and so I am intelligible to the world.

It strikes me always, in these moments, that if I could have that experience forever, if I could disappear into a normative heterosexual life, part of me would instantly do so. In these moments, I understand every trans person who went stealth even if they didn't "have to," I understand every stupid joke about men and women from every brainless comedian and sitcom writer I've heard since the womb—and I even understand the straight people who say marriage could only be between a man and a woman. I understand how they'd feel so strongly about it they'd believe it would sully their experience to open it to others. That this feeling might be so *good*, and, yes, *communal*, and what would bind me into it with others is something I want to keep *just that way*.

It's all so much more than just sharing something with a tiny group of people like me, such as trans-themed book tours or the precious island of a tight-knit workplace or the friendly, recursive populace of Windsor bars. What I'm talking about here, it's a feeling like I'm sharing something with *not a small group but the world*. The "reality" of which is beside the point; it *feels* this way to me.

This feeling is dangerous. This jolting wash of communal feeling, when I examine it (once I've come down from it), makes me think of certain other phenomena: Packs of men hooting at a girl in tight pants, knitting together brotherhood. My army friend in high school recounting his buddy turning to a visibly Muslim guy at the airport and saying, "Dirka dirka, motherfucker," and all of us laughing at his story, but more importantly, taking joy from it, for we all felt then in community—a true thing that happened no matter how much I hate thinking about it. In grade four, when we learned Canadian history, one of our class's favourite lessons was about how, during the War of 1812, Canadians went down to the US and burned down the White House.[*] We loved this story, we repeated it, we talked about it after class. This stuck with us, a class of mostly white Canadian children, and we remembered it over other things we learned, like the Red River Rebellion against the colonial state led by Métis leader Louis Riel and how our government executed him. Is it more than metaphor how closely steeped you can find the etymology of community and nationalism?

Sarah Schulman said about anti-gay prejudice: "Homophobia is not a phobia, it's a pleasure system. Whenever I looked into the eyes of someone being homophobic, they were not afraid, they were actually enjoying it."[85] (I hear my grandmother again on the town she loved, and the gay kid in it who wasn't just ostracized but was cause for laughter: "We used to...") Rick Moody once wrote, "I don't know why homophobia seems to be the single most important community-building principle of middle school life, but that's how it was at my school."[86] I doubt he wrote it completely as a joke. Schulman talked about the misnomer of words like *hate* or *fear* to describe homophobia; she focused instead on the concept of joy. One could spend a long time thinking of what's to be learned from all this.

....

[*] Itself a bit of neat fact-twisting on the part of my teacher. It was the British army that did this; "Canada" as a nation-state did not exist at the time.

II.

Compassion

MORGAN M PAGE once said, "Pay attention when people invite you to turn off your compassion. It happens all the time. But compassion isn't actually a finite resource."[87]

I think about that all the time.

Money is a finite resource. Time is a finite resource. Emotional energy—which is different from compassion—is definitely a finite resource. But compassion? No. Morgan's right.

I used to hear, in my circles, in the wake of someone being a shitty human: "That person is garbage." "I wouldn't piss on him if he was on fire." Usually the person in question had done something shitty, indeed. But rarely had this person done something so egregious as to warrant synonymity with literal trash. Yet I would hear this often, and sometimes I happily returned the shit-talking. When I did, I could see a fire grow with fuel—like, say, I did that night in high school when after a night of cathartic complaining I pulled up my keyboard and wrote to my friend A. To withhold compassion, especially on a community level—even when it seems as if there's plenty of reason—it's amazing how easy it is to do. Pay attention when you're asked to do it.

The idea of compassion as not being finite has helped me immensely. The key thing to unpick here, I think, is the difference between emotional energy and compassion. Emotional energy involves things you can't do forever or for just anyone, even if you'd like to—e.g., you can talk for hours with a friend going through a hard time, but can you do it deep into the night, or with multiple friends every day, or after coming home from a chaotic day at work, or when a stranger accosts you in the bar or the train? Sometimes, sure. Pervasively? Unlikely. Anyway, the questions of emotional energy, it's all the stuff of the hard questions of being a decent, stable human.

Compassion's a little different, though. I'm not sure you can run out of it in that way. I think it might be counterproductive to hoard it. When I encountered Morgan's words here, I was living in Windsor, and I was often angry at a certain housemate. I was also often angry at my ex-girlfriend with whom that years-long breakup took place. I was also angry at the literary industry I was working in, whose values did not always line up with mine. And I was angry at certain Mennonites who were clinging to transphobia in a manner that affected my personal life. I had good reason to be angry in all these cases! And I did not owe everyone in these equations my emotional energy or my time. But it didn't do anything for me, in the most literal manner, to not have compassion. It didn't cost me my dignity or self-respect to extend compassion—the way it might have, say, to extend emotional energy or time. Opening myself to compassion while maintaining boundaries, in such cases, actually helped me unstick myself from cycles of anger and move on.

Now. I do mean a lot in that last paragraph *personally*—I want to relate how this shook out for me and me only. With anger, for instance, I see plenty of friends and colleagues whose anger is pointed in productive, healthy ways, particularly in political settings. Amazing. If your anger keeps you on the side of the angels, bless you. For me, anger has not kept me on that side. Anger does not give me lasting fuel, it burns me out. Anger does not focus my energy, it exhausts it and makes me unkind to people I care about. I know that about myself, at this point in my life. And the idea of compassion as not finite—*not something to be hoarded*—helps.

Bringing it back to community, opening myself up to this concept of compassion allows me to expand conceptions of my communities away from insularity. Cliquishness. Suspicion towards outsiders.

Openness. It allows me to keep the borders of community in my life porous in a way I can only see as good. I think a lot about openness.

Activation

> Visceral private meaning is not easy to alter by
> oneself, by a free act of will. It can only be altered
> through exchanges that go beyond self-expression
> to the making of a collective scene of disclosure.
>
> Michael Warner,
> "Public and Private"[88]

THERE'S A POWER of community to actually change minds.
When I think about those few times in my life I've witnessed a person, be it myself or close friends, change
their own visceral private meaning solely by themselves,
solo and on their own, it is so exceptional that it proves
the rule.

I knew, for instance, in my early twenties that I had to
transition. Sometimes it is easy to tell that story with the
implication that I divined my path alone.

But though the experience was often lonely, that also
would not be wholly true. For one, I spent long hours
lurking on online message boards and stress-testing my
thoughts and desires against a community who did not
know I was there. But even more importantly, I made the
final decision to transition after witnessing and befriend-

ing a trans woman whom not only could I get along with but I saw interacting with friends, a partner, a bevy of acquaintances (say it with me now: a community). I can't overemphasize how that helped settle things for me.

Did I do a lot of it by myself? Sure, I did. But it's interesting, how appealing the bootstrap-notion of transition as one person's inner fortitude can be. That story has been put on me sometimes. I don't think it's the whole truth.

I also think of my mother and stepdad, who thrived in more secular communities rather than the religious ones in which they were raised. I saw them become who they needed to be as adults, I think, especially once I was out of high school, and I wonder if that was partly because of the new groups of people in which they found themselves. (I've just thought of that, writing this. That's a strange thing to consider.)

I'd posit that community can *activate* us in key ways that it is nearly impossible to do, as Warner says, through a free act of will. That activation can open us to larger worlds, and close us off to them too. And, sometimes, both at the same time.

Freedom

IN JANUARY 2022, anti-vaccine-mandate activists affiliated with the Canadian far right drove into the nation's capital of Ottawa. They called themselves the Freedom Convoy, and they gathered to demand the removal of all COVID-related mandates and governmental restrictions. Over a thousand vehicles took up downtown streets and gridlocked the city; at its height, as many as eighteen thousand people showed up in a day to protest.

The purported catalyst for the protest was the new mandate that truckers get vaccinated to do cross-border runs. Activism against *vaccines* themselves, though, was truly the centre of the protest, and the grosser brands of far-right activity were firmly threaded through the movement. Some Convoy organizers promoted QAnon and Christian nationalism (as well as plenty of its crowdfunders[89]) and had engaged in rampant Islamophobia.[90] Nazi and Confederate flags were visible in the crowd. Demonstrators danced on the Tomb of the Unknown Soldier and pissed on the National War Memorial. They harassed a local homeless shelter, demanding food and threatening their security guard with racial slurs.[91] Residents of downtown Ottawa experienced racist, homophobic, and sexual harassment when they walked around outside,[92] and many couldn't sleep because the truckers were setting off fireworks and honking their horns non-stop into the night.

Many Conservative MPs either said nothing about this or openly scoffed at the neighbourhood's denizens. "I'm right downtown ... I have my white noise app going on," said then interim Conservative leader Candice Bergen* when asked about the disturbances.[93] She also said there were "good people on both sides" of the Convoy, in an eerie call-back to Donald Trump's comments after the deadly 2017 white supremacist rally in Charlottesville, Virginia.[94] Conservative MP Pierre Poilievre full-throatedly endorsed the Convoy and blamed any "inconveniences" it was causing on Justin Trudeau. Poilievre now leads the Conservative Party of Canada and could quite possibly be our next prime minister.

All in all, it was about three weeks before the feds cleared the Convoy from Ottawa streets.

And during those weeks—in which the majority of the nation was infuriated and downtown residents lived menaced and sleepless—the Convoyers were having a grand old time! You might even call it a shindig. "As of Saturday afternoon, the protests were peaceful and there was a largely party-like atmosphere on Parliament Hill," observed the *Globe and Mail,* "with some people handing out cookies and coffee and others drinking beer and smoking marijuana." They set up bouncy castles for their kids. They set up barbecues. They played hockey. In a very telling choice of words, the *Daily Hive* wrote, "It was a show of old-fashioned Canadian nationalism."[95] One year after

* Who, fun fact, represented my old homelands of Manitoba's Pembina Valley

the whole mess, a protester reminisced, "We inspired the world . . . it made me proud to be a Canadian again."

As all this shit went down in Ottawa, a smaller tranche of the Convoy popped up at the US border in Windsor— right in our neighbourhood, about a twenty-minute walk from our house. They blocked off the Ambassador Bridge, the busiest single border crossing in North America,[96] across which one-quarter of Canada–US trade travels. As in Ottawa, the protesters brought kids. A line of children held hands across Huron Church Road, the thoroughfare that connects the bridge to the freeway system, and the road my housemates and I walk across to get groceries.

The cops cleared that one sooner; it lasted about a week. I wasn't in town, but my housemates were. After the first few days, they and friends went down to check out what the hell was going on while everyone else watched the Convoy livestream. We had a group chat.

Friend 1: *LAST NIGHT 10pm*
100 trucks, maybe 4 big trucks
20+ cop cars with their lights swirling made it festive, with the warm weather had a nice little street party feel for a few hundred revellers.
classic rock on speakers
tecumseh to mcdonalds NOTHING just a blocked off street
to quote the internet . . . if this had been Natives they'd have been bulldozed away on day2

Friend 2: *I honestly kind of want to go to the protest because I heard they're playing street hockey on Huron line . . .*

Friend 3: *that does sound fun lol*

Friend 1: *saw a dont tread on me flag but no swastikas*
the trucks are gone but theres still 350 people
now they playing volley ball

Friend 3: *mcdonalds is making* BANK

Friend 2: *This is totally a street party lmaooo*

Friend 1: *the crowd is growing*
the media is giving out food !!!!
free chocolate bars

Friend 3: *That was pretty big*
*I'd say there was like 1-2 thousand people all up and down
huron line*
*guys camping out and having a fire in the back of a semi truck
like a nativity scene lmao*
Big party at mcds
*Tecumseh is more people driving in circles and honking and
yelling. It seemed a little dangerous people walking on the
road and people driving on the road . . .*
*There was about 100 police cars all up and down huron line
and all the access roads are blocked. I saw a man in a swat or
sort outfit so I left (plus we had done all our gawking)*
Everyone there sounded kind of stupid and angry.

Friend 2: *It was like Pride . . . I just wanted to have a social
interaction*

Friend 1: *Looks more like Canada Day*

Friend 2: *Yeah except more American flags*

I think a guy tried to get me to stop and smoke weed with him but I'm not trusting a man hiding in the shadows under a bridge lol

A lot of freedom chanting. These people make me wonder if I should value freedom so much with how dumb they're being. Like I don't even know is this an anti vaxx protest or an anti lockdown protest or an anti Trudeau protest

Friend 1: *Live feed guy just kept saying* FREEDOM! *any time anyone looked at him*

(Hours later)

Friend 1: *its a dance party now*

Friend 2: *it was always a dance party*

A Part of Something

WHEN BENEDICT ANDERSON wrote on nationalism in 1982, he referred to the preceding few centuries as the era of "print capitalism," embodied by the act of reading a newspaper:

> The significance of this mass ceremony—Hegel observed that newspapers serve modern man as a substitute for morning prayers—is paradoxical. It is performed in silent privacy, in the lair of the skull. Yet each communicant is well aware that the ceremony he performs is being replicated simultaneously by thousands (or millions) of others of whose existence he is confident, yet of whose identity he has not the slightest notion. Furthermore, this ceremony is incessantly repeated at daily or half-daily intervals throughout the calendar. What more vivid figure for the secular, historically clocked, imagined community can be envisioned? At the same time, the newspaper reader, observing exact replicas of his own paper being consumed by his subway, barbershop, or residential neighbours, is continually reassured that the imagined world is visibly rooted in everyday life.[97]

I find it useful to consider communities as always having traces of anonymity—or perhaps at least the *possibility* of anonymity, of a new person you don't know coming in. I find it helpful to consider the lovely strangeness of that anonymity, as well as its power. And like the figurative newspaper in the barbershop or the subway, there's still so many tangible traces that bond us to others we don't know. From idly watching CNN break news at the gym, to hilariously relatable viral memes made by strangers, to a government emergency smartphone alert that sends everyone on the bus scrambling, to the Yankees winning the World Series—they won it my first fall in New York, resulting in an instant street party and someone setting a tree on fire (?)—to when the Oscars gave seven wins to *Everything Everywhere All at Once,* a movie I watched alone and loved to tears, and I felt, indeed, *reassured that the imagined world is visibly rooted in everyday life.*

In keeping with the paradox that community represents, we maybe all have our own respective versions of these communal experiences on both the tiniest and grandest scales—from, say, a small publishing house with a staff of six to something as vast and violent as a nation.

Anderson asked this question: "What makes people live and die for nations, as well as hate and kill in their name?" As he points out, some nationalist revolutions were initiated by the upper classes and the well-to-do. In, for example, the United States and Venezuela, it was the gentry, people who lived general lives of material comfort and security, who were willing to put their bodies on the line and go to war for their countries. And these stories, as I'm intimately acquainted with in the United States, are sometimes used for eons after to inspire young men to do the same. I can only imagine how the stories of the Convoy have so far reached young men across Canada, and beyond.

If we conceive of nations as another example of community, then this phenomenon is yet another example of community's *power*—power in the lower-case *p* sense that can be used for all kinds of goodness and ills, a peerless power that shows up in society again and again.

When I heard what the Freedom Convoy was like on the ground, I didn't find its festive atmosphere surprising. The Convoy differs from communities I cherish, but how different, really, beyond opposing views? I don't want to throw in my lot with pundit-brain centrism, I do not believe in "horseshoe theory" that the extreme left and right meet at their ends. I do indeed believe, plainly put, that the Convoyers believe fucked-up shit and I don't. What's beyond that, though?

There are many ways for the imagined world to be visibly rooted in everyday life. I suppose I'm saying that Anderson's book reinforced a lifelong hunch of mine. Something like: don't underestimate what it means to be part of something.

Assumptions (Final)

THIS ONE TIME on book tour, we stopped on the Jersey Turnpike for gas. It was summer and hot, a Northeast humidity-and-garbage hot, but I bought a regular coffee anyway because back then I didn't like it iced. The driver, an American, laughed. "I love that you're so Canadian you drink hot coffee even when it's like this."

I've never heard that assumption echoed by anyone else. But the bizarreness of that comment has always stuck with me. Like: many Canadians love iced coffee, I just don't. (Winnipeggers even have a thing for Slurpees in winter.[98] It's weird!) It also doesn't make sense. Wouldn't someone more immune to cold—another assumption—therefore enjoy colder drinks? This was a pretty low-stakes interaction, as far as Canadian stereotypes go.* But it stayed with me, and it revealed something to me.

In Kristin Dombek's book, she wrote on Adam Morton's essay "Empathy for the Devil":

....

* Which isn't to say they always are. The stereotype of Canada as nice, polite, and socially stable tends to paper over everything from racism and colonialism in our past and present to our increasingly rickety health care system. The term "maple washing" was coined about this.

When we try to understand others, Morton says, we inevitably do so from our own position, by comparison to ourselves. This point of view limits us to identifying "a small number of relevant factors, holding others implicit." We focus on those factors we recognize superficially and quickly from our own lives, but because we are so invested in viewing ourselves as "good," we often miss the most important ones. We do this constantly; we have to in order to live . . . And yet it is important that we do a better job of it, particularly when it comes to the devils among us.

Morton is talking about evil, about humans doing physically violent and cruel things—the opposite of an offhand remark about coffee and a nation-state. But what Dombek examines repeatedly is the consistency and rhythm of the "focus on the small number of relevant factors" when we try to understand others. "We do this constantly; we have to in order to live." We indeed must self-interrogate many such quick and easy comparisons. It's the stuff of being a good person and trying to make the world around us better. But not only can you not do it all the time, I wonder if such quick comparisons actually keep us sane and happy, a quiet metronomical ticking affirming to us that the world makes sense.

What struck me, with the hot coffee thing, was how intuitively this assumption made sense to my tourmate. It made *sense* to her. And moreover, she was visibly comforted as she laughed and said this, the assumption was clearly balming to her, the way assumptions are: as instant and human as farts, their examination necessary but their repression folly, there simply isn't time, they're part of how we manage the world, intractable material of the fabric of existence, something working on a deeper level, an imagined reality rooted in everyday life, impassively turning the Earth forward.

Awkward

IN THE EARLY days of COVID, some neighbourhoods banded together and helped each other get food, medicine, and health care, protected each other from eviction, and did all this safely. Such activities of mutual aid literally saved lives. And also—when you participate in such activities, on either end, sometimes you feel stronger and part of something. "As we enter the second month of the pandemic," goes a *Curbed* article from May 2020, "you may be feeling antsy or powerless—but there are plenty of ways to help your neighbors."[99]

The order of that sentence—"antsy or powerless" followed by "help your neighbors"—is not an accident. A reliable antidote to powerlessness and worthlessness is being part of a community that helps.

...and...well...letting yourself be helped.

Anne Helen Petersen recently wrote about this idea of "communities of care" specifically for those of us who tend to give care but not get it:

A lot of us are good at *giving* or being ready to *give* care. But we also need to be better at asking and receiving it, because all of this community work depends on divorcing ourselves from an understanding of anyone, anyone, as uniquely givers or receivers.[100]

That last point is really important. Understanding any one person, including yourself, as uniquely a giver or a receiver ... it's not very conducive to working together, to *being* together, no matter how benevolent one's aims. It just doesn't *work*, it's not how human interactions *work*. Modern capitalism can trick us into thinking otherwise, e.g., a workaholic ordering delivery so he can keep working isn't exactly taking part in a community of care, and he may perceive himself as "independent," but he is still dependent on food that someone else cooked. Even beyond that, though, metaphysically, the idea of "unique givers or receivers," as Petersen puts it, is just not how human interdependence operates.

When I think of the problem of "givers versus receivers," I think of Dombek's book again, and her careful rethinking of the false binary of narcissists versus empaths. For instance, some psychologists, from Freud on down, conceived of the narcissist as "a charming mask covering a cold calculator, a self empty of empathy and the capacity to love." But, Dombek reminds us, "others emphasized the role of self-love in narcissism, which Freud had, after all, called a normal part of human development; *they argued that self-admiration and care for others were reciprocal and mutually enhancing. The debates over narcissism were part of a larger argument about how we know and help other people at all.*"[101] (emphasis mine)

"Givers and receivers." It's a cutthroat binary at heart, almost copy-pasted from the hacks of electoral politics

("Makers vs. takers!"). It doesn't really reflect the complexities of how we as human animals move through a day in the world.

Some thoughts from Petersen as to why some resist recognizing themselves as *receivers* of care:

- "You haven't been around examples of healthy community or dependence—particularly within your family—and don't have models of what it means to safely ask for help."
- "The feeling that because of how your life outwards [sic] appears—'together,' 'without children,' 'without physical signs of illness'—that you shouldn't need help, because you have it so much easier than your friends/family who have ostensibly more 'difficult' lives."*
- "Previous attempts at reaching out for help have been rebuffed or ignored, and it hurt so much that you never want to ask again."
- "Simply not having the community or family or friend group that you feel comfortable enough to even ask for help in the first place."

It's all tough and all good food for thought, and the whole article on her Substack, "A Shortcut for Caring for Others (and Being Cared for Yourself)," is worth reading. Petersen had also asked her Instagram followers for specific examples of "ways they asked or offered help within their close or loose community." Some responses she shares in the post:

....

* Lordie, if I had a nickel for every time I've heard a variation of this one, quite often from people who are objectively really struggling/marginalized! It's a trap.

- Asking close friends to check on them at least once a week. "When my partner died I asked everyone to schedule calls with me so I could cry for an hour at a time."
- Offering last-minute child care. (Petersen added, "My offer text would say, 'Can I come hang out with your kids while you do some everyday shit?'")
- Offering to go grocery shopping for neighbours.
- A single mom of an infant identified 5 to 7 p.m. as the hardest time of her day, and she began asking friends to join her for dinner.
- To someone who suggested dropping off food for people who are sick or hurt or struggling, Petersen added, "I sometimes think it's really useful to just say 'I am dropping this off, what's the best time, we don't need to talk' instead of 'can I drop this off'."
- And then, a core suggestion of the article: a reader named Brenna said she made a little "user manual" of how she took care of herself and sent it to her closest friends and family (and asked them to make their own versions). This manual included "food that always tastes good, what reminders are most helpful, what poems/songs/movies always feel good, who we see for appointments, etc. It's been a few months and we've already been using them and it's such a good shortcut!"

Immediately, this last idea, of filling out a little guide on how-to-take-care-of-me and sending it to my loved ones—well, it struck me as VERY AWKWARD. It struck Petersen that way too, to which she said: "Sometimes community-building is awkward as hell."

And that is a sentence I will remember forever. Community building can be so awkward! It is often not exactly sexy! It can be mundane, dry, not immediately enticing or high-octane or cool. It's only in writing this essay, for instance, that I've remembered that while the Trans Lady Picnics were awesome, they were also SO DANG AWKWARD SO MUCH OF THE TIME. A fact that, well, sort of reinforced the need for them.

It is easy to forget these things. I'm reminded of Mira Bellwether again. "Here's what any of us can do differently: we can swallow our pride a little bit more and tell everyone how bad things are when they are bad. This doesn't ruin community, it's what creates community."

The responses to Petersen's Instagram question are all worth reading and provide nice examples of how to be part of something in a kind, secular* way. The link is in the endnotes.[102] Give it a look. Fingers crossed it's still up by the time you read this.

My favourite response of them all: "My husband got a job 90 minutes away—which wildly impacted our parental balance. My 5 year old son was stuck coming to his twin sister's dance class (which he did NOT like) until I asked our next door neighbors if they'd mind a little buddy for an hour or so once a week. They said yes! They're our age but don't have kids, and now my son loves his time next door and I feel like I have a little bit of that proverbial village."

....

* Many of those Instagram responses specifically bemoaned not being part of a religious tradition/community that might ameliorate some of the problems identified. The solution there, of course, is not "find religion" but to think about what you're missing that can maybe be built on your own. Like countless queers, for example, for whom families of origin did not work out well, the solution was to redefine and build a better kind of family in its place.

Queers

THEN AGAIN, COMMUNITY *can* be pretty sexy. Like, uh, literally.

I heard a line about activism once, whose origins I can't track down: "For it to work, people need to be getting laid." This idea works both literally and metaphorically. Literally because, well ... bitches got needs, and bitches with needs met can Do Shit. Metaphorically because people coming together to do a Thing have to *want* to be there. If it's cool, if it's fun, if it's a *good time,* you'll have more people and more Things will get done.

I used to oft-witness, in my personal circles, a romanticization of gay activism and struggles of the past, particularly among (though not restricted to) millennial and Gen Z queers like me who came of age in the twenty-first century. I have been part of many conversations valorizing groups like ACT UP (that's the big one) but others too, like Queer Nation and the Transsexual Menace. It happens easily. The subtext of these valorizations usually goes something like this: The queers that came before us were smarter and stronger. They were fearless and they didn't dodder around wasting time on frivolous things. They had their eyes on the enemy and they knew how to fight and win. And we? We do not do these things. We are frivolous and only focused on moping about our problems. Or something. I took part in many conversations where this is the subtext; I've started a few of them.

I don't hear this wistful romanticization as much anymore. Maybe it's my personal circles; maybe it was more a 2010s thing, before the backlash of this current decade; maybe it's both. Either way, I witnessed this romanticization a lot. And like: the history and lessons of these landmark activists are indeed important! And also, there's a story that often slips away, the one where people felt like they belonged and had a good time. Even in *United in Anger*, a documentary about ACT UP where reams of interviews and footage are crammed into a ninety-minute film—all while outlining some basics of AIDS politics and history—the filmmakers devote time to that feeling of belonging: "ACT UP became my whole social life." "ACT UP was very sexy. And I think that's one reason people wanted to be in on it." "The whole atmosphere of what act up was was a bubbling cauldron of tremendous political energy and ideas and action ... and flirting and cruising."

So that's pretty cool. Let's embrace doing things for fun and getting laid! Hell yeah. But.

Then there too is a question:

Why does simply saying the words *queer community* prompt reflexive recoil among many of my friends? Why does the very term cause a shrinking, a turning away?

True, queer community is often just fucking *awful*. Queer community can be exasperating, sad, mean, guilt-ridden, judgmental, whiny, passive-aggressive, and aggravating.

...and...

It doesn't just subjectively *feel* that way.

There is some rather disquieting research suggesting that the more queers are involved with our communities, the more we feel worse. Michael Hobbes from his landmark essay "The Epidemic of Gay Loneliness":

> Several studies have found that living in gay neighborhoods predicts higher rates of risky sex and meth use and less time spent on other community activities like volunteering or playing sports. A 2009 study suggested that gay men who were more linked to the gay community were less satisfied with their own romantic relationships.
>
> "Gay and bisexual men talk about the gay community as a significant source of stress in their lives," [Yale researcher John] Pachankis says. The fundamental reason for this, he says, is that "in-group discrimination" does more harm to your psyche than getting rejected by members of the majority. It's easy to ignore, roll your eyes and put a middle finger up to straight people who don't like you because, whatever, you don't need their approval anyway. Rejection from other gay people, though, feels like losing your only way of making friends and finding love. Being pushed away from your own people hurts more because you need them more.

Pachankis is at the centre of this research on what he calls intraminority stress. It used to be, the idea goes, that the wide disparities in mental health among queer populations—substance abuse, depression, suicide, you name it—were first homophobically attributed to pathology, and then, more recently, to trauma. Hobbes: "Gay men were being kicked out of their own families, their love lives were illegal. *Of course* they had alarming rates of suicide and depression."

But after a bit of careful attention and research, the trauma explanation began to wobble. These mental health disparities, researchers found, remained even among populations who had not survived homophobic traumas; and even among those who did, such traumas weren't what kept coming up. An uneasy source of stress came to light: ourselves. As a *Guardian* journalist described one researcher's work: "Local men in his studies rarely report, 'I had a really difficult week because someone called me a fag.' It's much, much more common that folks are talking about intraminority stressors of a lot of dating apps, judgment, and sexual racism within the community."[103]

Much of this research focuses on cis gay men and tends to finger the dog-eat-dog travails of masculinity as a culprit. Toxic masculinity undoubtedly exacerbates this stuff, sure, but I also can't help but think these lessons are applicable to wider queer communities—i.e., the phrase "dyke drama" doesn't come from nowhere, and dating app bullshit and judgment and sexual racism are not exactly unprevalent in lesbian and trans worlds, and speaking of which, ask any young lesbian what she thinks of the app Lex and be prepared for a deluge. In a broader sense, this is all age-old, and personally might I say that trans community infighting in my own life seems about as inexorably aggravating as New York traffic.

Beyond the world of Homoland, I also can't help but wonder if the idea of intraminority stress, while perhaps uniquely urgent and stakes-laden to queer people, can't apply to communities beyond ours, including those who are, politically speaking, not minorities. One early reader of this essay, for instance, shared with me her experience of similar trials in the world of comedy writing. "That community," she told me, "has made me who I am and also broken my heart and driven me away, over and over."

A characterization from Hobbes sticks with me: "Being pushed away from your own people hurts more because you need them more." *Because you need them more.* I'll buy that. I think often of Jo Freeman's 1976 essay "Trashing: The Dark Side of Sisterhood"[104] published in *Ms.* about feminist movement infighting: "The Movement seduced me by its sweet promise of sisterhood," Freeman writes. *"I gave the movement the right to judge me because I trusted it."* (emphasis mine) "And when it judged me worthless, I accepted that judgment." As an example of the nerve she touched, Freeman says the essay "evoked more letters from readers than any article previously published in *Ms.*" Like I said: age-old.

And yet—and yet! The attitude of "Okay, so it's not trauma, it's intraminority stress?"—that takeaway feels a little too pat as well.

As one lens among many, I think the idea of intraminority stress can be useful, but . . . I dunno. As the assault against trans rights ramps up in the United States, I find myself thinking: Is intracommunity drama *really* as devastating to our mental health as, say, getting our actual health care taken away, or even the spectre of same? Is the research fingering ourselves as culprits really so ironclad? That seems like quite the high bar to clear.

Intracommunity stress strikes me, perhaps, as a visible

and particularly painful symptom of poor mental health among queer people, but I wonder about being quick to focus on it as a cause. A friend reading over this essay suggested, "What if the problem isn't that I'm depressed in the [gay] neighbourhood; what if the problem is that I'm depressed for all these other reasons?" Maybe, she suggested, that's not the neighbourhood doing you wrong, but the idea the neighbourhood, on its own, is going to help you, period.

A JARRING SELF-DISCOVERY as I've written this: I personally don't feel intracommunity stress in my own queer life. Not anymore. I used to. I remember going to those old Trans Lady Picnics with some dread. They were life-giving and nourishing, and also anxiety-producing! I was certain I was stupid and boring; I was certain I had nothing to offer. It wasn't atypical of my early queer community interactions. Both at such events and online on social media, I was often out of my mind with anxiety about what specifically other trans women might think of me, women I thought were cool and smart and wonderfully loud. Their opinions about transness and how to move through the world would live in my head and follow me around, because I wanted to live up to these women and impress them and I thought myself too weak and milquetoast to do so. It was the kind of stuff that seems so silly now, but that stuff always does, and it was real. Like, an offhand intelligent remark articulating how they refused to let anyone call them "dude" could depress me and live in my head rent-free for weeks, because sometimes *I* let people call me "dude" and it annoyed me a little but I didn't care, and maybe that meant I was dumb for not realizing how bad it was to be called "dude" or how weak I was for letting people call me that anyway, which actually these women could *see on my Facebook wall people calling me dude, oh shit, were they talking about me?!* ...

That kind of thing, you know?

This occupied my mental energy all while none of these women were directly unkind to me! Did all this affect my mental health more than, say, the street harassment I was receiving at the time, much of which was actually aggressive? Hard to say, that's probably unanswerable. But my experiences definitely do match this idea of "intraminority stress."

And those are experiences I don't have anymore. It's funny, reading over the research, I've been nodding along with descriptions like Pachankis's and Hobbes's even though I currently don't feel that way *at all*.

Why did this happen? Why'd I chill? *When* did this happen, even? I can't pinpoint it. Maybe it's just a function of time. It's been over a decade since that first picnic. Maybe it's a function of what happened in that time, when I've seen a million people arrive and leave my queer communities. Maybe it's that some of them left because they died, and grieving the deaths of your friends can do things to your mind. Maybe it's that I've seen enough of those dreaded call-outs and "getting cancelled" (modern parlance for Freeman's "trashings," perhaps) to know that with a bit of persistence and good faith, life can go on after them. Maybe I've grown blasé to how queers can be awful to each other, maybe I'm wilfully not seeing bad things (i.e., maybe I *should* be more stressed). Maybe it's that I've moved around so much as an adult, and lived and worked in enough straight settings, that I'll always treasure being around a bunch of homos when I get to do that, and so I have faith we'll stick around. Maybe it's that I've lost some faith in queer communities' ability to shelter or guide me. Maybe it's that I've been lucky and privileged enough that most queers treat me nicely, and time has nothing to do with it. Maybe it's because I've spent a lot of my adult life attempting to do my part in queer communities, and there's something organic and mutually reinforcing about that, such that I've ended up solidly secure in my feeling of belonging.

All these contradictory-but-interlocking explanations feel plausible yet don't quite add up to a whole. But what's undeniably true is that the stress faded away at some point. Bully for me, I know. But it makes me skeptical about the inevitability implied in these writings on intra-minority stress (whether the writers intended that inevitability or not). Do we have to hate the idea of queer community? Do we have to be exhausted by it? Much of adult life involves recognizing mental anguish and finding ways out of it. I would posit, actually, that's a skill a lot of queers have! "Being pushed away from your own people hurts more because you need them more." Sure. But what if that's a retrospective discovery, not a law for the future? Can you need something without letting it hurt you? "I gave the movement the right to judge me because I trusted it." Can trust exist without the possibility of judgment? Maybe not, but these feel like questions with answers.

NOT THAT THOSE answers come easy. My own experience continues to befuddle me. Or, at least, hold some mystery.

* * *

MAYBE I'LL END this with one idea of Pachankis's I really love, which is about generation gaps:

> One thing that's often been underutilized in the gay community is intergenerational mentorship. And that works both ways. We know that LGBTQ+ older adults are more likely to be living alone, and that's a risk factor for depression. And we know that LGBTQ+ young people are, in most cases, not born into families that are also LGBTQ+, so they don't inherit a sense of the community, norms, or history from their parents. A perfect way to learn it would be fresh from the elders in our community; at the same time, elders in our community would probably benefit from contact with younger generations. There's historically been a lot of barriers to that, but to the extent that the gay community can lead the way in breaking down those barriers, I think that it would be a tremendous intervention against this type of gay-community stress across the full spectrum.[105]

I love the specificity of this idea, but I cite it too for its general spirit: figuring out how to nourishingly connect within our communities, having some faith that, despite constant trouble, connection is still better than disconnection, and brick by boring brick there are ways to find it. Jeremy Atherton Lin wrote in his book on queer nightlife: "If my experiences in gay bars have been disappointing, what I wouldn't want to lose is the expectation of a better night."[106]

Manageable

THERE ARE TWO cornerstone reasons I've invested my spare time in building trans-centred culture, specifically with writing and literature.

One reason is simply that trans people are a minority under frequent discrimination and attack, and we live more marginalized lives compared with the average population—the online shop Darknest has a sticker that drily reads "The trans agenda is an average life expectancy"[107]—and I want to do my part against such marginalization. I'm also much more of a cultural organizer than a political one. I'm not much of an activist in the make-demands or knock-on-doors or hold-the-line fashion (and I've tried). So it's my hope that such cultural community building can play some part in the nourishing of trans life in a time of trouble, even though I've seen it go wrong plenty of times.

I don't know how it'll pan out. But it's what I believe in and what I know how to do. I'm sticking with it.

Which is the second cornerstone reason. It's a world I ended up in and a world I can contribute to. It's a very unsexy, tangible, simple, and solid reason: it's what I ended up knowing how to do.

I am relaying these specific experiences, dear reader,

not because I want each of you to join me in trans cultural organizing, but to share how I have personally ended up making sense of all the frustrating, contradictory facets of community that I have been raising. To kick the tires on the concept of community . . . that means confronting tough questions. But the conclusions above are small, manageable things in my life and heart that I know. These conclusions make my life better, and they give me stuff I can do, ways to give my time to the world. Maybe you have your own small, manageable things in your life and heart that you know too?

Contributions

AS SHE WAS writing *Harlem Is Nowhere*, Sharifa Rhodes-Pitts observed a bunch of messages drawn in brightly coloured chalk on sidewalks along Lenox Avenue. They were messages like: "Youngsters can you print and spell?" "Think better to be a better person." "Give more and hate less." "Your life is worth saving." They would quickly wear away with foot traffic and rain, then reappear freshly drawn and new.

Rhodes-Pitts would incessantly copy down the sidewalk messages when she saw them. "Although they were designed to be destroyed," she wrote, "I felt compelled to preserve them." She assumed the chalk writer was "an old woman, a retired schoolteacher, continuing her educational mission with these sidewalk signs," but this was not the case. When she finally met the creator of the messages, he was wary of being written about, refusing to let her publish his name. "When I complimented him on what he was doing," she wrote, "he shrugged and said that he was only trying to make his *contribution,* and that this was something we all had to figure out how to do."[108]

Definitions

MICHAEL WARNER WROTE extensively on the idea of *publics*—his definition of which: "An indefinite audience rather than a social constituency that could be numbered and named."[109]

If I can relate his ideas about publics to mine about community,* take this part of one of his essays:

> This essay has a public. If you are reading (or hearing) this, you are part of its public. So first let me say: welcome. Of course, you might stop reading (or leave the room), and someone else might start (or enter). Would the public of this essay therefore be different? Would it ever be possible to know anything about the public to which, I hope, you still belong? What is a public? It is a curiously obscure question, considering that few things have been more important in the development of modernity.

....

* Warner might take issue with this, as his definition of *community* is explicitly narrower in scope, one that doesn't consist of strangers and where members have clear enumerations and recognitions of each other. I have a more expansive view of the term *community,* of which I think his definition of *publics* encompasses much, and I tend to think it's more semantics than substantial disagreement.

Publics have become an essential fact of the social
landscape; yet it would tax our understanding to
say exactly what they are.[110]

You may have noticed that so far I have not hazarded
a precise working definition of the term *community*. This
was intentional. Community is so slippery and heterogeneous a concept that I'm skeptical of anyone's ability to
come up with an authoritative definition for which there
wouldn't be an immediate slew of counter-examples. As
Warner says, "it would tax our understanding to say
exactly what they are."

I also wasn't sure, at this essay's outset, how useful
such a definition would be. I mean, most of us walk
around every day casually slinging around terms we
might struggle to firmly define if someone buttonholed
us on it, even as those terms involve weighty matters. You
don't always have to define something to make use of it,
or improve it, or even understand it.

Plus, important phenomena are often a bit enigmatic.
Warner says too about the workings of publics: "The
temptation is to think of publics as something we make,
through individual heroism and creative inspiration or
through common goodwill. Much of the process, however, necessarily remains invisible to consciousness and
to reflective agency."[111] Yeah. Invisible to consciousness.[*]
If you can't nail down a definition of something, sometimes it's better not to try too hard; you just end up
jamming a square peg in a round hole and mucking up
the whole bit. I did peruse some existing working defini-

---

[*] (Personally, I'm consistently intrigued how some attempts at building community alchemically catch fire and some never gather a spark.)

tions of *community* as I brainstormed this essay, but I found them lacking,* not really getting at the gestalt of it all. So, I'd intended to complete this without attempting such definitions. That is, until I read Warner's essay, and discovered a stray fragment of a sentence where he posits a public as: "an ongoing space of encounter."[112]

....

* Example: David M. Chavis and Kien Lee at the Stanford Social Innovation Review offer: "Community is both a feeling and a set of relationships among people." Yes, it is both those things, but that also describes nearly every human interaction, doesn't it? I know I've been pretty expansive about what *community* can mean, but I do think that's a bit *too* general. ssir.org/articles/entry/what_is_community_anyway

An Ongoing
Space of Encounter

AN ONGOING SPACE of encounter.

SPACE: A place where community interactions occur. The borders of this space can be fuzzy and perhaps exasperating, but you can name it. A café, a small town's main drag, a dozen employees on a retail floor that everybody hates, a bar, a union hall, the block you live on, a Facebook group, the Facebook feed.

ENCOUNTER: The interactions in such a space. Usually a mix of dynamic and static, new and repetitive—and hopefully never calcifying, perhaps, in one or the other.

ONGOING: This space of encounter is not a one-off. There is a dependable mix of other humans in this space, and within it: a past, present, and future all exist, all three.

Maybe we could define *community* as "an ongoing space of encounter." It's not perfect, but nothing will be. It might be the closest thing, for me.

Families

TWO YEARS AND change into COVID, Kathryn Jezer-Morton wrote about mothering in the post-vaccine era, and specifically about how she'd missed her children being in other homes:

> I mourn the passing of two prime years during which other adults could have been hanging out with my kids. And I, likewise, have missed two prime years of looking after my friends' kids. It's time to let some new freaks in, let *them* tell the kids to pick their socks up off the floor. (...)
>
> I believe other people have the ability to make my kids cooler and happier than they will be if left solely in my care. This isn't because I "suck" or whatever—I am confident in my ability to raise my children, don't worry about me. But I know that family life was never meant to be so self-contained.[113]

(Yeah. There's research on this too.[114])

I think a lot about when I was a kid, and my single parents were overworked or drifting. I spent reams of time around my extended family, family friends, my friends' families. In my memory, my parents expressed some regret around this, wishing the situation was different but for scant money and divorce. They were frenetic years—but I'm glad it shook out that way. Though I was an only child and didn't have many friends, I had a childhood where from the get-go I understood the world was large and there was a kaleidoscope of ways to exist in it, and I had to adapt and consider and take part in those ways to get by. I'm grateful for it.

Jezer-Morton brings up as a contrast to her ethos the gentle-parenting movement, which focuses on honouring every child's wants and needs, "learn[ing] to recognize and control [their] emotions because a caregiver is consistently affirming those emotions as real and important."[115] But, as Jezer-Morton writes:

> The gentle-parenting movement would seem to argue that children are so intelligent, so intuitive, that to diminish them in any way would be unfair. But what if their intelligence can be encouraged in other ways, such as observing their communities buzzing around them and having to figure out, by trial and error, how to find their place within them?

In my queer universe, we often use the term *chosen family*. This is meant in contrast to our *families of origin* or *bio families* and it refers to loved ones who are closer than friends, whom we take care of and who take care of us, in a committed and permanent way.

I like the term, and by this definition I have chosen family of my own. But I also think that at a certain age all family is chosen! Like: You choose to keep ties or you don't. Some people you need enough to handle the ugly parts; some people don't always prove themselves worth all that. Accordingly, plenty of us choose, sometimes, to sever ties with our family members of origin, for reasons both horrid and honourable.

In this light, family and community bleed into each other a bit. I think that's kind of a special thing. Much earlier in this essay I wrote, "Community is a vital but oft-neglected sibling of those rarefied entities that keep one away from isolation and despair; it rests right up there with cherished friends, a partner who loves you, a family of some stripe who love you back, a passion or commitment that gives you juice through the days." Another lens on that, perhaps, is that community can be glue sticking these entities together, and that it attains some of the qualities of such entities themselves.

More from Jezer-Morton:

> During the loneliness of the pandemic, I often fan-tasized about "community." Community as an imagined abstraction is pabulum made of our own hopes and ideas, but anyone who has ever volun-teered for anything knows that belonging to an actual community is a mess. Community is full of other people's bad ideas and awkward behavior. It's hard work, and it's not perfectly safe. People say and do hurtful things in a community, often with-out meaning to. But any sociologist working today will assure you that community is much safer than isolation.

Not safe, but *safer*. Yeah, that scans.

I'm moved by this whole essay of hers extolling the virtues of her kids regularly chilling around other people's rules. While in part this is just personal catharsis over reading positive descriptions of something matching my own childhood, I'm struck by both the tender hopefulness of her statements as well as the concreteness of them. Even when it's not driven by material necessity, it's something clear to *do*, exposing one's kids to larger publics (*their communities*, as she writes). And there are other good things in this: "One of the reasons I like having my kids' friends over," she writes, "is that it forces me to keep my grumpiness in check and sometimes sheds disinfectant light on my lesser habits." Sometimes I visit a friend—maybe someone in that chosen family—and upon stepping into the friend's apartment, they bashfully say, "You coming over gave me an excuse to clean." I love it when this happens.

Strangers

WARNER ALSO TALKED about strangers.

> In modern society, a stranger is not as marvelously
> exotic as the wandering outsider would have been
> to an ancient, medieval, or early-modern town. In
> that earlier social order, or in contemporary ana-
> logues, a stranger is mysterious, a disturbing
> presence requiring resolution. In the context of a
> public, however, strangers can be treated as already
> belonging to our world. More: they must be. We are
> routinely ordered to them in common life. They are
> a normal feature of the social. (...)
>
> A nation or public or market in which everyone
> could be known personally would be no nation or
> public or market at all. This constitutive and nor-
> mative environment of strangerhood is more, too,
> than an objectively describable *Gesellschaft**; it
> requires our constant imagining.[116]

This notion ties me back both to Anderson (the *imag-*

* A German noun meaning "social relations based on impersonal ties, as duty
to a society or organization."

ined world, visibly rooted in everyday life) as well as to Page's articulation that compassion is not a finite resource. For a community to be a healthy and nurturing place, for it to function well, there needs to be some kind of openness and possibility towards strangers. Unhoarded compassion is probably a good way to make that work long-term. Openness and compassion can maybe offer some guiding lights here. They make not only communities healthier but individuals as well. Waldinger again: "Talking to strangers actually makes us happier."[117] bell hooks again: "Enjoying the benefits of living and loving in community empowers us *to meet strangers without fear.*"[118] (emphasis mine)

It is so easy for communities to grow insular, suspicious, bitter. Evils like xenophobia dovetail with this a bit, and so do more mundane things—cliquishness, for example. (I don't want to falsely equate xenophobia with cliquishness—like, one is worse than the other—but I do wonder if they drink from the same stream.)

It is so easy for communities to grow insular, suspicious, bitter. And often this is for *very good reasons!* Mennonites, years ago, were suspicious of outsiders because we were persecuted and sometimes killed by them—and because they might tempt us from devotion to our faith and way of life. (And these two things, persecution and temptation, cannot so easily be separated, though it might seem that way to a secular outsider.) Strangers can be complicated; strangers can be very dangerous. Hell, anybody who's ever shown a female face to society—technically a majority of the whole damn world!—understands how complicated this calculus can get.

It is part of a difficult adult responsibility to find ways

for protection and openness to work together. It is part of a societal contract that necessitates their meshing.

And honestly, I think this is something that in our bones many of us know how to do.

Scene: A New Yorker is walking out of the subway. It's late. A stranger approaches her. The New Yorker tenses. The stranger calls out. What's she saying . . . ? *Ah.* And the New Yorker relaxes as she understands they are saying, "*IS THE 4 RUNNING?*" for the stranger is simply a fellow denizen asking about the damn trains. That tensed New Yorker has often been me, wary for many of the reasons women at night are wary and, being trans, for further reasons still.

When I first transitioned, I became quickly jumpier in urban environments, because the outside world was treating me . . . poorly. So, I began to ignore strangers far more often than I once did, especially men, and I did not always acknowledge people. Sometimes I did not acknowledge people in my own neighbourhood, people I would later wish I had befriended, because I needed their community in times of trouble (that trouble also being transphobia from different strangers) and I had rejected their attempts at outreach.

Eventually, I realized I was doing this: I was rejecting friendly outreaches because I was also experiencing the unfriendly kind. I eventually realized I was never going to pass as a cisgender woman, not dependably anyway. I looked into the future of this tendency I was developing to be fearful and avoidant of strangers and I saw only resentment and darkness. And the unfair thing about resentment is that it doesn't matter if its source is honourable or petulant, it makes you twisted just the same.

I knew I would have to walk around in this life as a visible transsexual woman in a world that did not understand such a thing, and that this would necessitate a wariness and defensiveness I'd hoped to avoid, perhaps for the rest of my life. But I also knew that a state of universal suspicion would be unlivable. I did not want a life where I had no wish to leave the house, and even if I did, not leaving the house was not an option at that point in my life.

So I changed. I began to walk around with a wary-yet-open attitude towards strangers, in the tired, balanced fashion that marks many a peaceable adult life learned the hard way. And that's how I've chosen to live and I don't regret it, including through my own shitty encounters since.

Some years ago, a man gathered his arm in mine while I was walking home and made me jack him off. That man was a stranger. This experience traumatized me. There've been a few others like him. I am aware of the stakes of this subject of strangers. Too, I know what it's like to walk around traumatized like this ... And yet, there's a different kind of stranger and they're glaring at you with a face that reads "You upset me" when you walk into a new room, because this person actively considers you a man and a pervert (or these days, "a groomer"). I know what it's like when a parent pulls a child away when you cross their vision. I know what it's like to walk so softly and quietly but be palpably feared in a manner that goes against every way you want to exist in the world. I know what it's like to extend grace and understanding to strangers and not receive those things back. I know what it's like for this to just be existence. It is so very easy to grow insular, suspicious, bitter. But even when divining protection, the solution cannot be to seal oneself off from people you have not met. I believe such a future holds only bleakness. I believe the research that says talking to strangers makes you happier. I believe it with all my heart. Some of my Mennonite ancestors still gave food and shelter to strangers who came to their door, even not knowing whether those strangers could cause harm. But they were in those spaces. They were in a community. They couldn't just not exist.

This is hard, this feels like maybe one of the hardest things I'm touching on in this whole essay. This is a real question of danger and safety (and the lurking, pretzelled question beneath it of who gets to *feel safe* versus *be safe*). I know you can't just wave off such traumas. I know such fears are real because violence is real, and I know so many of us carry its marks.

What I come back to is that, most of the time, you still get up in the morning and go to work the next day. In one fashion or another. That's what I mean when I say this is something that many of us know in our bones how to do. Some of the people in my life who are kindest to strangers are also survivors of intense, pervasive trauma. I know, this is hard, hard shit, and trauma isn't much for obeying guidelines or rules or sweeping statements. Unlike some of the conundrums I've tossed around in this essay, this one really lives in the body. This isn't to suggest such practices are as easy as "changing your attitude" or whatever. It's to suggest that balancing this duality of protection and compassion— of openness—is deeply possible in this life. Most of us got up in the morning and went to work the next day.

The cultural historian Joe Moran wrote with some stoicism on the question of strangers: "The heartening lesson is that this tension between caginess and openness has existed throughout human history. We generally find ways round it."[119] Yes. It is easy enough to grow insular, suspicious, bitter.

Lurking, Social Media Revisited, the Warnings of Utopia

A TRUE STRANGER, of course, is one with whom you have actually nothing in common. Is there a way to react in these instances besides putting one's guard up and moving on? Such thoughts can fray the mind.

"Can you have a community without homogeneity?" asked a friend of mine, the one who brought up being-depressed-in-the-gaybourhood. There was this idea, she observed, "that people get together, rich and poor, Black and white, and it's all great—it's kinda true, kinda not." Yeah. In the end, most people still cluster and hang out with people like themselves, particularly when it comes to race and class.

Dear ol' Robert Putnam described the city as "not a single tightly integrated community, but a mosaic of loosely coupled communities." I thought of this description when the above friend of mine wondered if there were answers in cosmopolitanism: "I think I want a world in which communities bump up against other communities," she said. That indeed feels more aligned with reality to me, or, at the very least, a more possible one.

In "... Three, Two, One, Contact: Times Square Red," Samuel Delany wrote, in the late 1990s, of New York City's Disneyfication of Times Square that was hollowing out the neighbourhood. In an echo of both Putnam and my friend, he said, "Urban contact is often at its most spectacularly beneficial when it occurs between members of *different* communities."[120] He uses this term, *contact,* to describe this chance kind of mixing—"the good Samaritans at traffic accidents," "the conversation that starts in line at the grocery counter." Delany begins the essay, "Given the mode of capitalism under which we live, life is at its most rewarding, productive, and pleasant when large numbers of people understand, appreciate, and seek out interclass contact and communication conducted in a mode of good will."

In a companion essay, "Times Square Blue," Delany wrote of his decades cruising for gay sex in the old porn theatres of Manhattan, before the city forced them to close. In summarizing these encounters—Delany also uses that word, *encounter*—which *did* take place across race and class, he said something beautiful, something that recognizes the boundaries of what such encounters, such urban contact, can have, and the mutual deepness of what they can give to a life (several lives, a city, a community):

Despite moments of infatuation on both sides, these were not love relationships. The few hustlers excepted, they were not business relationships. They were encounters whose most important aspect was that mutual pleasure was exchanged— an aspect that, yes, colored all their other aspects, but that did not involve any sort of life commitment. Most were affable but brief because, beyond pleasure, these were people you had little in common with. Yet what greater field and force than pleasure can human beings share? More than half were single encounters. But some lasted over weeks; others for months; still others went on a couple of years. And enough endured a decade or more to give them their own flavor, form, and characteristic aspects. You learned something about these people (though not necessarily their name, or where they lived, or what their job or income was); and they learned something about you. The relationships were not (necessarily) consecutive. They braided. They interwove. They were simultaneous ... These relationships did not annoy or in any way distress the man I was living with—because they had their limits.[121]

Limits.

I'VE BEEN THINKING again about how social media fits in all this. As I'm writing this section, in May 2023, Twitter has been steadily self-destructing (in *my* circles at least) under the leadership of Elon Musk, and the alternative network Bluesky is rising in popularity. More research is coming out all the time that social media has deleterious effects, and its effects among youth—the ones who don't remember life before it!—seem particularly bad.[122] Some research suggests that those who use social media to *complement* face-to-face interactions don't have as many bad mental health outcomes, but those for whom social media is the *only* way they engage with others,[123] and/or for those whose use is excessive, upwards of five hours a day,[124] that's where social media's real ill effects lie.

I do wonder, though. This world is still so new, and new technology is so dependably fingered as a harbinger of loneliness and disconnection. (*Bloom County*'s melancholy around cable TV, *Sula*'s lamentation of the telephone.) Like, okay: Let's take someone who mostly connects through social media, and doesn't have real-life communities: that seems bad. In another era, would not that person maybe be zoning in front of the TV all day? Would that really be better? I'm sympathetic to the idea that our social media feeds might be cooking our brains, but I'm skeptical it's as simple as "less of that, please."

The idea of lurking, particularly, is of interest to me. On its face, lurking seems not so communal, maybe even a little sad—scrolling from the sidelines, never posting or interacting, just watching. But I think, sometimes, there are lovelinesses buried in this action. There's that one good trans message board I lurked on for years, barely ever commenting, and I learned and grew a lot through that lurking; it helped me dive into the adult trans life I had to live. My friend from comedy-world told me that she'd recently got into Reddit, and she's mostly lurking, she's found some subreddits she likes reading, it's a nice punctuation to her day. I can't help but think, too, of the lonely kid I was, cruising video game forums and finding people on AIM. It might sound a little glum, sure, but the question remains—what's the counterfactual? There's that line from Emily Zhou's story again: "You can almost feel normal ... like you're a member of some chorus, no matter what's going on with you." This resonates with me.

Some research points to the rise of algorithms as a way to unpick this knot—e.g., on platforms like Facebook and Twitter, the algorithm points your eyeballs to the things most likely to cause emotional reactions, and the point of these companies is to make money and they make money when you keep scrolling and clicking, and what's making you scroll and click often induces rage or despair. These algorithms can be invoked for everything from, say, the depression crisis in teen girls—psychologist Jean Twenge talks of young women "going down rabbit holes of negative content, and then not being able to reset because the algorithms think this is the content you want to see"—to exacerbating racial hatred and stoking death, like in Sri Lanka, where bursts of Islamophobic violence were linked back time and again to Facebook's newsfeed.

With this lens, it's not that social media *creates* these issues—e.g., depressed teen girls and hate violence are not uniquely modern problems—but that it *turbocharges* them. A Sri Lankan presidential adviser said in 2018, "The germs are ours, but Facebook is the wind, you know?"[125]

Maybe this is also a bit too easy. But anecdotally speaking, I can see their point. Some old-school social media that never depended on algorithms, like LiveJournal or MySpace, felt a lot calmer. While drama certainly existed on those platforms, it was nothing like the experience of, say, opening Twitter to respond to a message and instead getting blasted with a rando's outrages that I never asked to look at. Conversely, I've been enjoying some Discord channels lately where this isn't a problem.

I wonder, accordingly, if blaming "social media" for such ills is too impossibly general, when the design and raison d'être involved in various platforms can vary so widely. Part of the Facebook story in Sri Lanka is that Facebook officials were repeatedly presented with the problem and took no action. The problem, then, is not "social media" writ large, the problem is individuals who committed corporate malfeasance, and who were not willing to fix their product, even as it encouraged death.

John Herrman has described Twitter as "basically a system in which millions of people are constantly interrupting each other."[126] Can't we design systems that don't do that? What would such a product look like? What if we had social media platforms that might eventually meld into the fabric of a life in a less inflammatory, more convivial way, in a way that one day might leave us going *Water, what the hell is water?* That, too, feels attainable. Not assured, not even likely, honestly. But ... attainable.

I DID END up talking to my uncle, the small-town principal, about that moment years ago when he ran out of gas and passersby swooped in to ferry him to work, the one who had expressed of his adopted hometown, "I've lived there twenty years, and I still don't feel like I'm *from* there." I sent him a draft of this essay and he read the whole thing. I asked him about that moment. Did he feel differently that day?

"You've got the story right," he wrote me. "Wow, that was embarrassing. I think I was too embarrassed to 'feel like I was from there' at that time. Running out of gas means bad planning... to have had that on public display was, again, embarrassing."

(Thanks for letting me share it anyway in these writings, uncle, I appreciate that.)

We talked more about all this over Zoom. He's retired now, and he moved back to the Steinbach region, one house over from where he grew up. He talked to me as he was repainting my grandfather's house (rest in peace), the one my uncle and my mother and their siblings grew up in, in the Southern Manitoba village of Mennonites that is, strikingly, continuing to grow.

He also wrote to me:

Your life compared to mine is very different for many reasons. I'd imagine that living in a city of such overt diversity like NYC makes nearly anyone wonder where and how they belong. Community can become a fleeting concept. It's much different than living in a small town and, for those who do that kind of thing, belong to the same church as most of those around them. *Community of a sort is a given in those small-town environments.* (emphasis mine)

At the beginning of this essay, I'd wondered if his running-out-of-gas experience was more "Water, what the hell is water?" where, if functioning community is an intrinsic part of life, you don't think about it much, you've got other concerns. I guess I got my answer: yes.

With what he said about living in NYC: the experience he's talking about is my experience, that of transplants with no connection to an ethnic or cultural group that exists there. But I keep coming back to that thing—the way community might be threaded through our lives in ways so firmly we don't fully comprehend it.

"CAN YOU HAVE a community without dissonance?" is a question my uncle put to me. (A question I might intertwine with my friend's: "Can you have a community without homogeneity?") He also found it funny reading of my mother's attempts to meet our new neighbours in the suburban Northwest. "Around here, you know, it's just…" He gestured. "Know your neighbours? Of course."

My uncle's a recent cancer survivor, and he commented further:

> In the past few years, I've joined the cancer "community." There are Facebook and Instagram groups that focus on this topic and the many subtopics about cancer. It's an interesting international community that transects culture, political persuasion, etc. It's a group of people hoping for hope. It has made me realize that there are so many "communities" that people are part of…it takes endless forms.

That it does.

Belonging

TOWARDS THE END of my writing this essay, my editor raised the subject of *belonging*. "Isn't it, in one way, what community is all about?" he asked me. He went on:

> And isn't it this aspect of community that brings out both the best and worst in its individual and/or collective members? How does it feel *to feel* as if you belong to a given community?…Or, conversely, how does it feel *not* to belong, and why, often, does one feel that way…We often talk about communities keeping people out, as othering, whether these be outsiders, strangers or undesirables; but sometimes it's the members or would-be members themselves who self-ostracize.

Yeah. One wonders. The opposite, I suppose, of *feeling a part of something*. Again: Where does community exist in life that's a given, where one doesn't even realize or feel it, where you might feel compelled to say, "I don't feel like I'm *from* there," yet in very practical senses you are? If I gotta be honest, when my friend at that party in my hometown, years ago, intervened with the snarling dude

("It's cool, he's from here"), I hadn't really *felt* like I was *from* there either. But that didn't matter. My own *What the hell is water?* moment, I suppose.

When my editor brought up this question of self-ostracization, I thought again of people in my life fearful of "being cancelled" who, well, keep not getting cancelled. Or Anne Helen Petersen pointing out that sometimes you're bad at receiving care because you haven't been around good examples of such, or "previous attempts at reaching out for help have been rebuffed or ignored, and it hurt so much that you never want to ask again." Like my editor says, sometimes it's the would-be members themselves who don't let themselves in. Not all the time. But sometimes. It's a thing. It's a thing that happens. What to do about that.

I think there's a symbiotic yet intense difference between the subjective *feelings* of community, which we could call belonging/not belonging—as well as the way we can protectively, reflexively talk ourselves out of it—and then the objective *actions* of community, the workaday interchange of care and joy and gossip and cruelty and beers and ignorance and shunning and underwear washing and commiseration and love, all of which you can realize is happening, or you can not.

Coffee

WHEN I WAS beginning to drink coffee, I accidentally bought whole beans one day and didn't realize the "you need to grind them" part until I got home. I didn't grow up with coffee in the house. I posted on a local LiveJournal community to be like, "Help, any ideas, are there other ways?!?" (I was twenty years old, bless me.) And someone with a spare grinder at home asked for my address and drove to my apartment and dropped it off. She insisted. She just ... did it. I saw this person in a flash at my doorstep in a blur of thanks and then she was gone. I never saw her again.

Is there a strange possible chance you're reading this? I've never forgotten the sensation of opening my door to you, a stranger, your hand outstretched with the unsolicited gift.

Some Things I Know

THERE ARE SOME concrete things I know, certain ideas I can live by that I don't want to give up on.

Communities are healthiest when they make room for the private and the public.

Neighbourhoods and small towns are such ready-made models for community in part, perhaps, because their infrastructure accommodates private and public lives. They can contain parks, sidewalks, shared fences, schools, corner stores, coffee shops (Tim's!), bars, grocery stores—all places that may flexibly encourage public interaction and support. And they contain private homes to which the residents can withdraw from public if and when they choose.

In messy reality, of course, it doesn't always work that way. Miriam Toews wrote in *Swing Low* of her parents telling the neighbours, decades ago, that they were expecting a child, and the neighbour responded: "I've known you were pregnant for ages, Elvira, because you haven't been opening your curtains first thing in the morning." The book, told in Toews's father's voice, continues: "Elvira, of course, was vomiting first thing in the morning, while the curtains stayed shut for an extra ten minutes ... It's nearly impossible to break news in a small town. Some might say that's part of a small town's charm, and some might not."[127]

The tension of private and public is an ongoing push and pull. Today, I find myself being a very public person, who also hears and keeps many private secrets.

I keep thinking of Jezer-Morton talking about "passing my kids and their friends back and forth among houses." A community of different kinds of families can variously make their homes function as both solitude and communal refuge, a mélange of public and private that can accommodate that community's needs. I hold that as an aspiration of how the public and private of a community can be conjoined and mutually reinforcing. The calibration's never perfect, but it's an aspiration worth keeping.*

Communities sustain with serendipity and labour—which both, also, must be sustainable.

A lasting community needs forces within it doing work to make it last, and a lasting community has to have *some* room for serendipity. Maybe even a bit of chaos.

An open mic night is an easy example. It'll probably happen in a bar or café, where attendees run into and meet each other and talk before and after the show. But even, say, a stuffy membership meeting in an old-fashioned organization has time for idle chit-chat around the room before and after. In church, it was the communal lunches and weekly Bible studies and serving other members in need that built community as much as, if not more than, Sunday morning services. (When I talk with

....

* Delany wrote of this too: "When social forces menace the distinction between private and public, people are most likely to start distrusting contact relations."

the many apostates in my life for whom religion is no longer an option or a good thing, it's often those aspects of community I hear as being missed.) A sustainable, thriving community cannot exist without room for random, organic interactions. Serendipity is the oxygen that lets community breathe and last.

And labour. Happenstance, fleeting communities can exist with minimal effort. (This is one of those things I think social media is actually *good* at.) But sustainable, resourceful communities—less so. I've seen so many eager souls over the years bite off more than they can chew out of good intentions, and projects fail out of the gate. If you don't have a plan, overwork and overextension are as dependable as the winter. When the sex worker–run magazine *$pread* went on a staff retreat after a year in business, one of their agenda items went: "how to avoid burnout and hating each other."[128] Smart! So many beautiful things go under because the labour involved wasn't sustainable. If the labour can't sustain, neither can the thing.

Communities can't be all things. It is good when communities are wise to their capacities.

Communities aren't panaceas; they aren't everything, as expansive as my definitions of them have hoped to be. They're small, necessary things to which we all are bound.

Bryn Kelly, one of those first trans women I met in New York (rest in peace), wrote a Tumblr post years back about how organizers can make events more welcoming. In one part, she talked specifically about accessibility and being explicit and upfront about what a physical space can and can't provide:

Just be honest. Not every space can accommodate
every body ... the more information they have, the
more opportunity they have for communication
with you ... Ultimately, I think often, people would
rather know exactly what they're getting into, even
if it's imperfect (again **no space is safe and perfect for everyone**) than have something bill itself
as an ALL INCLUSIVE ANTI-EVERYTHING-IST FAIRY
WONDERLAND and have people come and find out
it is *definitely not that.*

Good advice for any event organizer, and that last bit,
about billing events as an "all inclusive anti-everything-ist
fairy wonderland," sticks with me. She's poking a bit of
fun at the social justice–oriented lefty events that tend to
use impossibly broad language, of course, but there's a
deeper horizon there too. You can say of your gathering:
"All are welcome." But are all *truly* welcome? Probably
not. What would it take to make everyone welcome? Is
that in your capacity? No, really ... *is it?* It's often not.
That can be a starting point. My uncle also observed to
me: "An essential element of community seems to be
trust, of one kind or another."

Communities will always benefit from asking themselves,
"What do we not want to look at? What makes us uncomfortable
to think about? What do we quietly find ourselves wishing away?

This is, I think, a remedial bulwark against community
strength being exercised for cruelty, perhaps one of few
available.

By definition, examining what you don't want to think
about is a difficult task, hard to pin down. But it's rare you
regret it. I often think of critiques of the publishing

ecosystem, for example, critiques I share but I'm also part of. When I notice myself annoyed by those critiques, sometimes I am quick to feel defensive, and often for very good reason. But there's nearly always good reason to be annoyed by critique! It's worth it to ask these questions anyway: *What do I not want to look at? What do I wish would just go away?*

It's worth it even more to ask and think through these questions in the company of others.

Communities should strive for openness, a continuous ability to welcome visitors and potential new members.

Policed borders breed insularity and suspicion; within them compassion so easily withers. It is tough when you have to be careful who you trust. It's tough when safety is a factor. But when a group makes itself purposefully small and grows ever smaller ... it can become a photocopy of the isolation that community would otherwise dispel.

In the end, if I aspire to distinguish what separates the communities I hope for from the Freedom Convoy or Christian nationalists in North Idaho, if I try to get beyond the tautologies on which such attempts often depend (e.g., "They believe fucked-up shit, and I don't"), I think there might be a distinction in *openness*. With openness and potential for both visitors and new members, there comes grace and possibility. Imagined communities, to use Anderson's term. Contact, to use Delany's. Strangers, to use Warner's.

Presentism! It's bad.

It's easy to slip into the language of stasis. The conversations I have about community feel oft-underpinned by the assumption that trends will march forever on—I'm thinking of Opus despairing about cable TV again—that certain machinations are etched in titanium. My stepdad once told me that when indoor smoking bans began hitting society in the seventies and eighties, people were worried it'd undermine chit-chat at the office! Funny. Even now, in the year it's taken me to write this essay, you can take a bus from Windsor to Toronto again. Two companies have opened up routes. Cheapest is $39.99 one-way on FlixBus, ouch. (I guess it's still 2023.)

Still none for those Southern Manitoba winter highways, though.

Trends that seem bleak or inevitable do sometimes hold. But sometimes they don't. That Starbucks on Third Avenue still has no place to sit down, but that's not every coffee shop. I wrote part of this section in a café in Manhattan with a pack of chattering young people at the table in front of me and a sullen, lone weirdo drawing at the window in the corner opposite. (Bless you, lone weirdo.) Back up in Windsor, that Tim's by our house still keeps their dining room open. You can still sit in it round-the-clock for a two-dollar coffee. I sold an old e-reader on Facebook Marketplace the other day; the buyer and I met there to complete the deal because, duh, where else? I sat there with a bagel and read afterwards, as the denizens and passersby of our neighbourhood drifted in and out.

WHEN THOSE "THIRD spaces" do close, it can really get me down. I can over-extrapolate it to something huge, sinister, and unending. When, of course, I have no idea how the future's going to go. I have trouble reminding myself of that sometimes. But I do believe it, it's true.

Even as it also means the future could be so unimaginably worse. I could go to that Tim's right now if I wanted, as I'm putting the finishing touches on this essay. It's open and I'm back in Windsor for the summer. Also, wildfire smoke is making going outside dangerous for even a few minutes, so, well, I'm at home. The unknown does tend to humble.

THERE'S ONE OTHER story I want to share, something I'm moved by: The first doctor I had when I came back to New York was a cis gay guy, well versed in stuff like trans health care and PREP, who seemed to have a pretty nice gay-doctor New York life. Last fall he moved back to Texas, where he was from, amidst an onslaught of state-wide attacks on access to, well, trans health care and PREP. "They need good doctors there," he said.

I hold him in a lot of esteem. There's much I assume about him and his life when I do. Assumptions again, I know. And a state government's brute force can brush aside any one person's good intentions like dust.[129]

Still. I think about him. I know what he said, "They need good doctors there," and I know he was a good doctor and I know he's now gone from New York. Those things are real. (Rhodes-Pitts's chalk messenger speaking of contributions, "something we all had to figure out how to do.")

An Arrow

TALK GETS CHEAP and life's not that long. I have been neglecting certain attentions to my communities lately because, uh, I've been writing this essay about community. An irony with its own lessons, I suppose. And my own life needs attention, I've been realizing as I write this, and I haven't been letting my communities help how they might. Though the other day I had an emotional meltdown about my future—pardon the vagueness—and I wrote about that in a tizzy, online, where only a couple of dozen people could see. Some of those people blessedly reached out. I'm glad I made that meltdown somewhere a small community could hear. Most of us have limited resources, all of us limited time.

When Tracy K. Smith reviewed *Harlem Is Nowhere,* she said:

> Every seismic social shift originates in someone's kitchen or living room with the decision to cease doing something that only recently had felt perfectly normal, or to accept the necessity of an action that had seemed impossible, unthinkable.[130]

What to do with limited time? For me, on a day-to-day basis, I can feel an arrow inside my mind pointing me towards decisions that lead towards better community, less isolation. Sometimes I fucking hate those decisions and they're hard, but when I really calm myself and let myself sit with them, I usually know which decisions are the right ones.

In the spirit of the subject, I'll end this by telling you all about a thing, something I initially told myself I didn't want to share in this writing: That communal house in Windsor I belong to? I never wanted it to be that way. Right now my ex, Sybil, and I share the place with three other people. If you told me, when we bought the house, that that would be the situation it turned into, I would've thought it a nightmare. I never wanted something like this; I have always wanted to live either solely with a partner or alone, which currently isn't the case in New York, where I teach during the school year, or Windsor, the place to which I come home.

What happened was this: We bought this house in summer 2016 back when Windsor still had old-time Rust Belt prices. We miraculously found a house we could afford that we didn't have to fix up. We moved here, celebrated, and then almost instantly broke up. Neither of us had the dough to buy the other out, and we really didn't want to sell it; back then we figured this had been our one shot at home ownership, and if we sold it and parted ways, we'd never have that chance again.

As is perhaps expected over seven years of running a house with your ex-girlfriend, this house has witnessed a galactical level of interpersonal turmoil, fighting, screaming, extraordinary bitterness and rage and pain. It's the kind of situation that from the outside I might have scoffed at in more cynical times, seen all that fighting and pain and gone, *Wow, what a bunch of drama. All under one roof? Not for me, no way.*

But we ended up sticking with it, and it's become one of the neater things in my life. I've had to reorder what I thought I needed out of that life. And the breakup in question wrecked my brain in so many ways. Too, if the unforgiving mechanics of home ownership had not forced our hand, this never would've happened—like, if we'd been renting, I would've definitely peaced out long ago. I relate all this to connote the chaotic, remarkable serendipity of how this house came together. For me, I suppose at some point I indeed accepted the necessity of an action that had once seemed impossible, unthinkable. We've been having big movie nights in the backyard with our friends and their friends in summer. Most of us are trans and queer weirdos, though not all. My dad lives in the next neighbourhood over, after many life trials of his own, and we all go out to the local together. He got sick last Christmas and I went over with Sybil—who, today, is still my best friend—and we brought him pie. I think the house will be around for a while. We're planning on that, though of course, who knows. It's ended up one of the best things about my life, and yes, it's nurtured a little community, with no small element of imagination and mystery.

There is an arrow inside my mind that gently tells me, over the course of my days, which decisions lead towards better community and which do not. Like the afternoon eleven years ago when I called in to work and went to that Trans Ladies Picnic with a bag of shitty chips. *That* one's truly wild to think about—that project has since spread all over the world! I didn't fucking know that would happen then, and somehow I was both participant and witness to its beginnings. It felt so impossible that afternoon to call in and go to that picnic, but I did. What else can I do that now seems unthinkable? And what about you? Don't give up on it. Don't give up on this stuff.

Acknowledgements

THANKS TO THOSE whose probings, suggestions, and encouragement helped me write this. A deep well of gratitude in particular to Juanita Doerksen, Harold Peters, Jackie Ess, Garth Doerksen, Nathan Dueck, and Dan Wells for their prolonged, gracious, and incisive discussions about this material. Thanks go also to Cat Fitzpatrick, Jonathan Dyck, Lauren Herold, Elvina Scott, Sharon Pfaff, and once again the best writing group: Megan Milks, Craig Willse, Hazel Jane Plante, Carley Moore, and Caitlin Kunkel.

Thanks to the Biblioasis crew—funny life to be on the other side of those desks! Big ups to Emily Mernin, Ashley Van Elswyk, Jodi Tremblay, Emily Stephenson-Bowes, Madeleine Maillet, Vanessa Stauffer, and Dan Wells again, without whose prodding I would never have written all this out.

Thanks to the staff at PLAYA—Carrie Hardison, Kris Norris, and Shawna Negus, who generously provided space in the Oregon high desert to work on this at a frustrating time.

Thanks to the beautiful weirdos I lived with as I wrote this—Kate, my roommate in New York, and Sybil, Kiki,

Amilcar, and then-Gwen and now-June, my housemates in Windsor. The dream at Ye Olde House of Lamb Sandwich shall never die.

Thanks to all my communities—near, old, far, and future.

Endnotes

1   Porter, Ryan. "Casey Plett on Truth, Fiction, and the Illusion of Community." *QuillandQuire*, 17 Aug. 2021, quillandquire.com/authors/casey-plett-on-truth-fiction-and-the-illusion-of-community

2   Feder, Sam, director. Disclosure, *Netflix*, 19 June 2020, www.netflix.com/title/81284247

3   Hochul, Kathy. "Statement from Governor Kathy Hochul on Black History Month." *The Official Website of New York State*, 1 Feb. 2022, www.governor.ny.gov/news/statement-governor-kathy-hochul-black-history-month

4   Nguyen, Rosie. "DACA recipients urge Congress to act on immigration reform on program's 10th anniversary." *ABC13*, 15 June 2022, abc13.com/daca-dreamers-deferred-action-for-childhood-arrivals-10th-anniversary/11963244

5   Biden, Joe, and Kamala Harris. "Remarks by President Biden and Vice President Harris at Signing of H.R. 8404, the Respect for Marriage Act." *The White House Briefing Room*, 13 Dec. 2022, www.whitehouse.gov/briefing-room/speeches-remarks/2022/12/13/remarks-by-president-biden-and-vice-president-harris-at-signing-of-h-r-8404-the-respect-for-marriage-act

6   Otterbein, Holly, and Madison Fernandez. "The Overlooked Constituency Both Parties Are Now Targeting in the Georgia Runoff." *Politico*, 26 Nov. 2022, www.politico.com/news/2022/11/26/georgia-runoff-asian-american-turnout-00070827

7   "The Chappelle Controversy Tests Netflix." *The Journal from Gimlet Media and The Wall Street Journal*, 21 Oct. 2021, www.wsj.com/podcasts/the-journal/the-chappelle-controversy-tests-netflix/129544cd-6b4b-4ebf-8bce-688b4e246003

8   "Herman, Jody L., et al. "How Many Adults and Youth Identify as Transgender in the United States?" The Williams Institute, June 2022, williamsinstitute.law.ucla.edu/publications/trans-adults-united-states

9   Lang, Nico. "Caitlyn Jenner: Donald Trump Is a Champion for Women and LGBT People." *Advocate*, 29 June 2016, www.advocate.com/election/2016/6/29/caitlyn-jenner-donald-trump-champion-women-and-gbt-people

10 https://twitter.com/majortransceleb/status/1626388187311648771 [tweet has been deleted]

11 Naga, Noor. *If an Egyptian Cannot Speak English,* Graywolf, 2022.

12 Whang, Oliver. "A Rural Doctor Gave Her All. Then Her Heart Broke." *New York Times*, 19 Sept. 2022, www.nytimes.com/2022/09/19/health/doctor-burnout-west-virginia.html

13 Reynolds, Mark. "'Harlem Is Nowhere: An Ingenious Weaving of History and Experience." *PopMatters*, 16 Sept. 2011, www.popmatters.com/148142-harlem-is-nowhere-by-sharifa-rhodes-pitts-2495957932.htm

14 Ellison, Ralph. "Harlem Is Nowhere, by Ralph Ellison." *Harper's Magazine* Archive, online 10 July 2014, harpers.org/archive/2014/08/harlem-is-nowhere-2.

15 Rhodes-Pitts, Sharifa. *Harlem Is Nowhere: A Journey to the Mecca of Black America*. Little, Brown and Company, 2011, p. 102

16 Anderson, Benedict. *Imagined Communities: Reflections on the Origin and Spread of Nationalism*. Verso, 2006, p. 6.

17 Anderson, *Imagined Communities*, p. 26.

18 Rhodes-Pitts, *Harlem Is Nowhere*, p. 79.

19 United States Census Bureau. "Sissonville CDP, West Virginia." *Explore Census Data*, data.census.gov/profile?g=1600000US5474356.

20 Kingson Bloom, Jennifer. "If You're Thinking of Living In/Marble Hill: A Bit of Manhattan in the Bronx." *New York Times*, 23 July 1995, www.nytimes.com/1995/07/23/realestate/if-your-thinking-of-living-in-marble-hill-a-bit-of-manhattan-in-the-bronx.html

21 Lao, David. "Greyhound Canada closure will be a 'disaster' for rural communities, experts say." *Global News*, 13 May 2021, globalnews.ca/news/7860104/greyhound-closure-disaster-communities

22 Rodriguez, Jeremiah. "Indigenous, rural residents left 'more isolated' after Greyhound leaves Canada." *CTV News*, 25 May 2021, www.ctvnews.ca/canada/indigenous-rural-residents-left-more-isolated-after-greyhound-leaves-canada-1.5442354

23 "community is a verb." *Twitter*, twitter.com/search?q=%22community%20is%20a%20verb%22&src=typed_query&f=live

24 "#communityisaverb." *Instagram*, www.instagram.com/explore/tags/communityisaverb

25 Weichel, Andrew. "Almost 200 pizzas arrived at warming centres across Vancouver this week. Here's what happened." *CTV News*, 23 Dec. 2022, bc.ctvnews.ca/almost-200-pizzas-arrived-at-warming-centres-across-vancouver-this-week-here-s-what-happened-1.6207579

26 Samatar, Sofia. *Tender*. Small Beer Press, 2017, p. 229

27 Thom, Kai Cheng. "Righteous Callings: Being Good, Leftist Orthodoxy, and the Social Justice Crisis of Faith." *Medium*, 8 Aug. 2017, medium.com/@ladysintrayda/righteous-callings-being-good-leftist-orthodoxy-and-the-social-justice-crisis-of-faith-ad89ee4f5b33

28 Hage, Rawi. *Stray Dogs*. Knopf Canada, 2022, p. 6

29 Frame, Selby. "Julianne Holt-Lunstad Probes Loneliness, Social Connections." *American Psychological Association*, 18 Oct. 2017, www.apa.org/members/content/holt-lunstad-loneliness-social-connections#:~:text=Not%20many%20people%20willingly%20cop,may%20hurt%20your%20self%2Desteem

30 "Loneliness and Social Isolation Linked to Serious Health Conditions." *CDC*, n.d., last reviewed 29 Apr. 2021, www.cdc.gov/aging/publications/features/lonely-older-adults.html#

31 Weissbourd, Richard, et. al. "Loneliness in America: How the Pandemic Has Deepened an Epidemic of Loneliness and What We Can Do About It." *Making Caring Common Project*, Harvard Graduate School of Education, Feb 2021, mcc.gse.harvard.edu/reports/loneliness-in-america

32 Druke, Galen. "The Politics of Loneliness." *FiveThirtyEight*, 2 Feb. 2023, fivethirtyeight.com/features/politics-podcast-the-politics-of-loneliness (It's about forty-nine minutes and change in.)

33 Keohane, Joe. "The Surprising Benefits of Talking to Strangers." *The Atlantic*, 4 Aug. 2021, www.theatlantic.com/family/archive/2021/08/why-we-should-talk-strangers-more/619642

34 Hwang, Tzung-Jeng, et al. "Loneliness and social isolation during the COVID-19 pandemic." *International psychogeriatrics* vol. 32, no. 10, 2020, pp. 1217–1220, www.ncbi.nlm.nih.gov/pmc/articles/PMC7306546

35 Walsh, Colleen. "Young Adults Hardest Hit by Loneliness during Pandemic, Study Finds." *Harvard Gazette*, 17 Feb. 2021, news.harvard.edu/gazette/story/2021/02/young-adults-teens-loneliness-mental-health-coronavirus-covid-pandemic

36 hooks, bell. *All About Love: New Visions.* William Morrow, 2018, p. 129.

37 Del Rey, Lana. "Ride." *YouTube*, 12 Oct. 2012, www.youtube.com/watch?v=Py_-3di1yxo

38 Auxier, Brooke. "64% of Americans say social media have a mostly negative effect on the way things are going in the U.S. today." *Pew Research Center*, 15Oct.2020,www.pewresearch.org/fact-tank/2020/10/15/64-of-americans-say-social-media-have-a-mostly-negative-effect-on-the-way-things-are-going-in-the-u-s-today

39 Zhou, Emily. *Girlfriends.* LittlePuss Press, 2023. p 72.

40 Breathed, Berkeley. "Bloom County." *Washington Post Writers Group*, 12 Nov. 1988, www.gocomics.com/bloomcounty/1988/11/12

41 Levitz, Eric. "No, Teen Suicide Isn't Rising Because Life Got Objectively Worse." *Intelligencer*, 23 Feb. 2023, nymag.com/intelligencer/2023/02/teen-suicide-depression-girls-social-media.html

42 Uda, Rachel. "In Such a Connected World, Why Are We Lonelier Than Ever?" *Katie Couric Media*, 6 Feb. 2023, katiecouric.com/health/mental-health/why-are-americans-lonelier-pandemic-social-media

43 Santos, Laurie. "Why Americans are lonelier and its effects on our health." *PBS*, 8 Jan. 2023, www.pbs.org/newshour/show/why-americans-are-lonelier-and-its-effects-on-our-health

44 Ortiz-Ospina, Esteban. "Is There a Loneliness Epidemic?" Our World in Data, 11 Dec. 2019, ourworldindata.org/loneliness-epidemic

45 Morrison, Toni. *Sula.* Plume, 1982. p. 166.

46 Putnam, Robert. *Bowling Alone Revised and Updated: The Collapse and Revival of American Community.* Simon & Schuster, 2020, p. 96.

47 Cross, Katherine Alejandra. "When Social Media Presents Only an 'Unlivable Life.'" *Wired*, 17 Apr. 2023, www.wired.com/story/twitter-trans-rights

48 Murthy, Vivek H. "Surgeon General: We Have Become a Lonely Nation. It's Time to Fix That." *New York Times*, 30 Apr. 2023, www.nytimes.com/2023/04/30/opinion/loneliness-epidemic-america.html

49 Wright, Talen. "Being trans and feeling lonely: a reflection on loneliness literature, community connectedness, and mental health in the transgender and gender diverse community." *University College London*, 28 July 2020, www.ucl.ac.uk/psychiatry/sites/psychiatry/files/talen_wright_blog_2020_07_28.pdf

50 Heinz, Matthew. "Communicating While Transgender: Apprehension, Loneliness, and Willingness to Communicate in a Canadian Sample." *SAGE Open*, vol. 8, no. 2, 2018, p. 215824401877778, https://doi.org/10.1177/2158244018777780

51 @TheeBellwether. "I helped get a trans woman out of jail once, who I didn't know and would never meet again. I made sure she ate well that night, and with another trans woman, in a strange city. Our collective ability to make things happen is real. It changes lives." *Twitter*, 22 Jul. 2022, 11:33 p.m., twitter.com/TheeBellwether/status/1550685566211170305

52 *A Safe Girl to Love*, since re-printed by Arsenal Pulp Press in April 2023.

53 Krajeski, Jenna. "This Is Water." *The New Yorker*, 19 Sept. 2008, www.newyorker.com/books/page-turner/this-is-water

54 https://www.tsqnow.online/post/t4t-triptych-the-concept-the-erotic-and-the-technique [bad link/expired domain]

55 Binnie, Imogen. "Notes on Nevada: Trans Literature and the Early Internet." *The Paris Review*, 4 May 2022, www.theparisreview.org/blog/2022/05/04/notes-on-nevada-trans-literature-and-the-early-internet

56 Plett, Casey. "The Novel That Started the Trans Literary Revolution." *Harper's BAZAAR*, 31 May 2022, www.harpersbazaar.com/culture/art-books-music/a40152169/the-novel-that-started-the-trans-literary-revolution

57 Stewart, Sophia. "Catapult to Shutter Online Magazine, Writing Classes." *Publishers Weekly*, 14 Feb. 2023, www.publishersweekly.com/pw/by-topic/industry-news/publisher-news/article/91526-catapult-to-shutter-online-magazine-writing-classes.html

58 @AEOsworth. "I literally taught last night! And I didn't know this was happening! I'm a little fucked up!" *Twitter*, 14 Feb. 2023, 11:50 a.m., twitter.com/AEOsworth/status/1625537950522941440

59 Samatar, Sofia. "Why You Left Social Media: A Guesswork: Sofia Samatar." *Catapult*, 29 Nov. 2017, catapult.co/stories/why-you-left-social-media-a-guesswork

60 Barnes, Brooks. "The Billionaire's Daughter Knows What You're Thinking." *New York Times*, 23 Feb. 2023, www.nytimes.com/2023/02/23/business/elizabeth-koch-perception-box.html

61 books.catapult.co

62 Steverman, Ben. "New York Gay Bars Are Declining—and Covid Isn't All to Blame." *Bloomberg.Com*, 24 June 2022, www.bloomberg.com/news/articles/2022-06-24/new-york-city-gay-bars-struggle-to-open-amid-red-tape-general-decline

63 Grabar, Henry. "Why Fast Food Is Racing to Ditch the Dining Room." *Slate Magazine*, 9 Sept. 2022, slate.com/business/2022/09/fast-food-drive-thru-mobile-ordering-mcdonalds-taco-bell-starbucks-dunkin.html

64 Haddon, Heather. "Americans Are Gobbling up Takeout Food. Restaurants Bet That Won't Change." *The Wall Street Journal*, 28 Jan. 2023, www.wsj.com/articles/americans-are-gobbling-up-takeout-food-restaurants-bet-that-wont-change-11674882022

65 Finkel, Michael. "The Strange Tale of the North Pond Hermit." *GQ*, 5 Aug. 2014, www.gq.com/story/the-last-true-hermit

66 Walker, Harron. "Cecilia Gentili Opens Her Burn Book." *Vulture*, 3 Nov. 2022, www.vulture.com/2022/11/cecilia-gentili-opens-her-burn-book.html

67 Johnson, Chelsey. *Stray City: A Novel*. Custom House, 2018, p. 205.

68 @intermittentcat. "I got skills, I met a lot of interesting people, and above all, I dragged myself out of a deep depression about the meaninglessness of my life that I had previously been experiencing." *Twitter*, 28 Jul. 2022, 4:12 p.m., twitter.com/intermittentcat/status/1552748742679347201

69 Mascarenhas, Natasha. "Launch House Raises Millions to Launch Houses (and the next Big Startups)." *TechCrunch*, 19 Aug. 2021, techcrunch.com/2021/08/19/launch-house-raises-millions-to-launch-houses-and-the-next-big-startups

70 Jennings, Rebecca. "Failure to Launch." *Vox*, 11 Sept. 2022, www.vox.com/the-goods/2022/9/11/23340917/launch-house-sexual-assault-web3-community

71 Haines, Josh. "How Launch House Is Redefining the Global Community."

ABC Money, 23 Jan. 2023, www.abcmoney.co.uk/2023/01/how-launch-house-is-redefining-the-global-community/.

72 *Zenger News*. "Decentralized Venture Capital: A Web3-Focused Launch House Debuts $10 Million Fund." *Forbes Magazine*, 22 Aug. 2022, www.forbes.com/sites/zengernews/2022/08/19/decentralized-venture-capital-a-web3-focused-launch-house-debuts-10-million-fund/?sh=1da871441c62.

73 www.launchhouse.com. Accessed 18 Aug. 2023.

74 Nguyen, Terry. "Why Brands Are Obsessed with Building Community." *Vox*, 30 June 2022, www.vox.com/the-goods/23186958/brand-building-community

75 Widdicombe, Lizzie. "The Rise and Fall of WeWork." *The New Yorker*, 6 Nov. 2019, www.newyorker.com/culture/culture-desk/the-rise-and-fall-of-wework

76 Hess, Amanda. "The Wing Is a Women's Utopia. Unless You Work There." *New York Times*, 17 Mar. 2020, www.nytimes.com/2020/03/17/magazine/the-wing.html

77 Fischer, Molly. "What Was the Wing?" *The Cut*, 15 Feb. 2021, www.thecut.com/2021/02/what-happened-to-the-wing.html

78 Walters, Daniel. "North Idaho Rep. Heather Scott Reaps the Glory—and the Consequences—of Being One of Matt Shea's Biggest Allies." *Inlander*, 2020, www.inlander.com/spokane/north-idaho-rep-heather-scott-reaps-the-glory-and-the-consequences-of-being-one-of-matt-sheas-biggest-allies/Content?oid=19045888

79 Jenkins, Jack. "How Big Christian Nationalism Has Come Courting in North Idaho." *Religion News Service*, 23 Feb. 2023, religionnews.com/2023/02/22/how-big-christian-nationalism-has-come-courting-in-north-idaho

80 Redekop, Magdalene. *Making Believe: Questions about Mennonites and Art*. University of Manitoba Press, 2020, p. xviii

81 Matthew 18:20, NIV.

82 Toews, Miriam. *A Complicated Kindness*. Knopf Canada, 2004, p. 89.

83 Blackburn, Venita. *How to Wrestle a Girl: Stories*. MCD x FSG Originals, 2021, p. 79.

84 *Johnson, Stray City, pp. 119–120.*

85 Maroon, Everett. "'Conflict Is Not Abuse' Changes Our Relationship with Confrontation." *Bitch Media*, 1 Nov. 2016, www.bitchmedia.org/article/conflict-not-abuse-activism-book-interview-sarah-schulman.

86 Moody, Rick. "Connecticut." *State by State: A Panoramic Portrait of America*, edited by Matt Weiland and Sean Wilsey, Ecco, 2009.

87 @morganmpage. "Pay attention when people invite you to turn off your compassion. It happens all the time. But compassion isn't actually a finite resource." *Twitter*, April 27, 2017, 10:15 a.m., https://twitter.com/morganmpage/status/857599129165455362

88 Warner, Michael. *Publics and Counterpublics*. Zone Books, 2002, pp. 62–63.

89 Lecaque, Thomas. "Leaked 'freedom Convoy' Donor Comments Clearly Demonstrate Christian Nationalist Presence." *Religion Dispatches*, 8 Mar. 2023, religiondispatches.org/leaked-freedom-convoy-donor-comments-clearly-demonstrate-christian-nationalist-presence

90 "Transcript: Unpacking Rhetoric of the 'Freedom Convoy.'" *TVO Today*, 3 Mar. 2022, www.tvo.org/transcript/2693255

91 Bilefsky, Dan, and Vjosa Isai. "Justin Trudeau Condemns Convoy Protesting Pandemic Restrictions." *New York Times*, 31 Jan. 2022, www.nytimes.com/2022/01/31/world/canada/trudeau-truckers-anti-vax-protests.html

92 Molina, Kimberley. "Fearful Ottawa Residents Flee Downtown as Protest

Drags on." *CBC News*, 8 Feb. 2022, www.cbc.ca/news/canada/ottawa/downtown-residents-flee-home-protest-fears-1.6341652

93 Lum, Zi-Ann. "Canada Invokes Unprecedented Emergency Measures—and Triggers a Political Firestorm." *POLITICO*, 2 Feb. 2022, www.politico.com/news/2022/02/14/canada-emergency-measures-political-firestorm-00008896

94 McGregor, Glen. "Bergen Pushed O'Toole to Back Convoy Saying There Are 'Good People on Both Sides': Sources." *CTV News*, 4 Feb. 2022, www.ctvnews.ca/politics/bergen-pushed-o-toole-to-back-convoy-saying-there-are-good-people-on-both-sides-sources-1.5768337

95 Laube, Aly. "Three Strange Things at the Ottawa 'Freedom Convoy'." *DH News*, 6 Feb. 2022, dailyhive.com/vancouver/ottawa-freedom-convoy-barbecues-bouncy

96 Oganga, Jeff. "This Is the Busiest International Border Crossing in North America." *The Travel*, 5 Dec. 2022, www.thetravel.com/is-ambassador-bridge-the-busiest-international-border-crossing-in-north-america

97 Anderson, *Imagined Communities*, p. 35–36.

98 Cadloff, Emily Baron. "How One of Canada's Coldest Cities Became the Slurpee Capital of the World." *Thrillist*, 3 June 2019, www.thrillist.com/eat/nation/winnipeg-slurpee-capital-of-the-world

99 Plitt, Amy. "How to Help Your NYC Neighbors during the Coronavirus Pandemic." *Curbed NY*, 14 May 2020, ny.curbed.com/2020/4/8/21213395/coronavirus-new-york-city-neighbors-how-to-help

100 Petersen, Anne Helen. "A Shortcut for Caring for Others (and Being Cared for Yourself)." *Culture Study*, 13 Nov. 2022, annehelen.substack.com/p/a-shortcut-for-caring-for-others

101 Dombek, Kristin. *The Selfishness of Others: An Essay on the Fear of Narcisissm*. Farrar, Straus, and Giroux. 2016. p. 48.

102 Anne Helen Peterson. "Give / Ask 4 Care." *Instagram*, 2023, www.instagram.com/stories/highlights/17912291885566319

103 Ryan, Benjamin. "Pressure to Keep up: Status Imbalance a Major Factor in Stress in Gay Men." *The Guardian*, 29 Feb. 2020, www.theguardian.com/world/2020/feb/29/gay-men-stress-journal-mental-health

104 Freeman, Joreen. "TRASHING: The Dark Side of Sisterhood." *Jo Freeman. Com*, www.jofreeman.com/joreen/trashing.htm

105 Kumar, Naveen. "The Gay Community's Obsession with Status and Looks Has Huge Mental Health Costs." *Them*, 7 Apr. 2020, www.them.us/story/gay-bi-racism-looks-grindr-anxiety-depression

106 Lin, Jeremy Atherton. *Gay Bar: Why We Went Out*, Back Bay Books, 2022, p. 10

107 Trans Agenda Sticker. Darknest, darknest.art/products/gay-agenda-stickers-trans-agenda-stickers-lgbtq-merch

108 Rhodes-Pitts, *Harlem is Nowhere*, p. 175.

109 Warner, *Publics and Counterpublics*, p. 56–57.

110 Warner, *Publics and Counterpublics*, p. 65.

111 Warner, *Publics and Counterpublics*, p. 14.

112 Warner, *Publics and Counterpublics*, p. 90.

113 Jezer-Morton, Kathryn. "Oxygenate the Family Unit." *The Cut*, 30 May 2022, www.thecut.com/2022/05/oxygenate-the-family-unit.htm

114 Reupert, Andrea, et al. "It Takes a Village to Raise a Child: Understanding and Expanding the Concept of the 'Village'." *Front. Public Health*, vol 10:756066, 11 Mar. 2022, https://doi.org/10.3389/fpubh.2022.756066

115 Winter, Jessica. "The Harsh Realm of 'Gentle Parenting.'" *The New Yorker*, 23 Mar. 2022, www.newyorker.com/books/under-review/the-harsh-realm-of-gentle-parenting

116 Warner, *Publics and Counterpublics*, pp. 75–76.

117 "The Politics of Loneliness." *FiveThirtyEight Podcasts*, Feb. 2, 2023, fivethir-tyeight.com/features/politics-podcast-the-politics-of-loneliness

118 hooks, *All About Love*, p. 143.

119 Moran, Joe. "Remember Hand Shakes and Small Talk? The Lost Art of Living with Strangers." *The Guardian*, 10 July 2021, www.theguardian.com/books/2021/jul/10/remember-hand-shakes-and-small-talk-the-lost-art-of-living-with-strangers

120 Delany, Samuel R., and Robert F. Reid-Pharr. *Times Square Red, Times Square Blue 20th Anniversary Edition*. New York University Press, 2019, p. 127.

121 Ibid, p. 58.

122 Hart, Benjamin. "The Grim New Consensus on Social Media and Teen Depression." *Intelligencer*, 8 May 2023, nymag.com/intelligencer/2023/05/the-grim-new-consensus-on-social-media-and-teen-depression.html

123 Putnam, Bowling Alone, p. 96.

124 Kelly, Yvonne, et al. "Social Media Use and Adolescent Mental Health: Findings From the UK Millennium Cohort Study." *EClinicalMedicine*, vol. 6, 4 Jan. 2019, pp. 59–68, https://doi.org/10.1016/j.eclinm.2018.12.005

125 Taub, Amanda, and Max Fisher. "Where Countries Are Tinderboxes and Facebook Is a Match." *New York Times*, 21 Apr. 2018, www.nytimes.com/2018/04/21/world/asia/facebook-sri-lanka-riots.html

126 Carmon, Irin. "What's an Ex–Abortion Doctor in Alabama to Do?" *Intelligencer*, 23 June 2023, nymag.com/intelligencer/article/alabama-abortion-dr-yashica-robinson-roe-v-wade-dobbs-anniversary.html

127 Toews, Miriam. *Swing Low*, Knopf Canada, 2000, pp. 41–42.

128 *$pread: The Best of the Magazine that Illuminated the Sex Industry and Started a Media Revolution*. Feminist Press, 2015, p. 22.

129 Carmon, "What's an Ex–Abortion Doctor in Alabama to Do?"

130 Smith, Tracy. "Harlem Is Nowhere: A Journey to the Mecca of Black America by Sharifa Rhodes-Pitts – Review." *The Guardian*, 11 Aug. 2011, www.theguardian.com/books/2011/aug/11/harlem-is-nowhere-review-tracy-smith

CASEY PLETT is the author of *A Dream of a Woman*, *Little Fish*, and *A Safe Girl to Love*, the co-editor of *Meanwhile, Elsewhere: Science Fiction and Fantasy from Transgender Writers*, and the publisher at LittlePuss Press. She has written for the *New York Times*, *Harper's Bazaar*, the *Guardian*, the *Globe and Mail*, *McSweeney's Internet Tendency*, the *Winnipeg Free Press*, and other publications. A winner of the Amazon First Novel Award and the Firecracker Award for Fiction, and a two-time winner of the Lambda Literary Award, her work has also been nominated for the Scotiabank Giller Prize.